The Bah

Don Philpott

Acknowledgements

My grateful thanks to all the very many people who helped me research and write this book. In particular I would like to thank Anita Johnson and Grace Hart-Hill of the Bahamas Tourist Office in Aventura, Florida, and Donna Francis in the Nassau headquarters, as well as Helen Fillmore of the Bahama Out Islands Promotion Board for all her splendid work, Greg Munnings of Coral Island, and Craig Stewart of the Underwater Explorers Society.

Dedication: To Pam, my beautiful American Rose

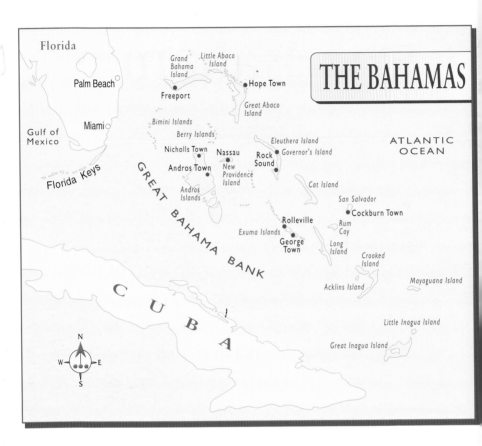

THE BAHAMAS

Florida

Grand Bahama Island
Little Abaco Island

Palm Beach

Freeport

Hope Town

Great Abaco Island

Gulf of Mexico

Miami

Bimini Islands

Berry Islands

Nicholls Town

Andros Town

Nassau

New Providence Island

Rock Sound

Eleuthera Island

Governor's Island

ATLANTIC OCEAN

Florida Keys

GREAT BAHAMA BANK

Andros Islands

Cat Island

San Salvador

Cockburn Town

Rolleville

Rum Cay

Exuma Islands

George Town

Long Island

Crooked Island

Acklins Island

Mayaguana Island

C U B A

Little Inagua Island

Great Inagua Island

N
W   E
S

The Bahamas

Don Philpott

• FEATURE BOXES •

Introduction

Almost nothing can prepare you for your first glimpse of The Bahamas as you fly in over the islands. The beautiful islands are set in a sea so blue and clear that even from the air you can see large fish swimming. The islands themselves are everything you could expect, with wonderful palm-fringed sand beaches ranging in shade from golden to pink. There are luxurious hotels and casinos and centuries old markets and historic buildings. The waters are generally safe and the sea warm, offering world class fishing, diving and sailing. There is a wealth of watersports, the freshest of seafood and other traditional Bahamian fare, festivals and regattas, and above all, a people that will welcome you with open arms.

BAHAMIAN HOT SPOTS

- **Nassau's Parliament Square** for history, architecture and atmosphere
- **Ardastra Gardens** for the tropical plants and marching flamingoes
- **Changing of the Guard at Government House** for pomp and pageantry
- **Eleuthera** for its fabulous pink beaches
- **Rand Nature Centre**, Grand Bahama, for traditional habitats and wildlife
- **Walkers Cay**, Abaco Islands, for world-class fishing
- **Andros**, great diving with the Tongue of the Ocean and the world's third largest barrier reef
- **Alice Town**, Bimini, the perfect place to get away from it all
- **Cat Island**, great scenery, beaches and the Hermitage
- **Exuma**, for the National Land and Sea Park, the first of its kind in the world.

… and before you go

Make sure that you have adequate insurance, and have packed the sun tan cream and sunglasses.

LOCATION AND LANDSCAPE

The islands of The Bahamas lie in shallow waters on a submarine plateau in the Atlantic Ocean to the north of Cuba and Hispaniola, and east of Florida.

The name Bahamas comes from the Spanish *baja-mar* which means shallow sea, and off some islands it is possible to safely wade out for hundreds of yards and never get out of your depth. Although the islands lie in shallow waters, there are deepwater channels to the south and west. There are almost 700 islands and cays (pronounced 'keys') in the group although only about 20 of these are inhabited, and more than 2,400 rocky outcrops breaking the surface. The islands stretch for more than 760 miles (1223km) from Grand Bahama Island which is about 50 miles (80km) off the south-eastern coast of Florida, south-eastwards to Great Inagua Island which is just 60 miles (97km) off the eastern end of Cuba and the Greater Antilles, the most northerly of the Caribbean islands.

The land area of all the islands is about 5,382 sq miles (13,939sq km), although The Bahamas covers 100,000 sq miles (259,000sq km) of the Atlantic Ocean, an area twice as large as Florida, larger than Britain and half the area covered by France or Spain.

The overriding impression about the islands is their flatness. Many do not rise more than a few feet above sea level, and the highest point on Bimini is only 20ft (6m) above the water. Beneath the fertile soil, there is a deep layer consisting of coral and the skeletons of other sea creatures, built up over millions of years before the islands were heaved up from the sea floor. Some of the islands exposed to the Atlantic have a ridge of hills on their north-eastern sides, although these are for the most part, large sand dunes, which in some areas have become compressed over thousands of years to form Bahama limestone. There are some limestone hills over 100ft (30m) high on Eleuthera and Long Islands, but the highest point in The Bahamas is on Cat Island with the tallest hill rising to 206ft (63m).

Because of the low elevation there are no rivers, although there are quite large lakes on some of the islands, especially Great Inagua, New Providence and San Salvador, and a substantial inland creek system on Andros. Offshore there are impressive reefs, and The Bahamas account for about five per cent of the world's coral resources, a remarkable figure especially when you consider that Australia's Great Barrier Reef contains less, with about four per cent of the world's coral.

HISTORY

COLUMBUS AND THE SPANIARDS

The Commonwealth of the Bahamas is a former British colony that gained its independence in 1973. The Bahamas were 'discovered' by Christopher Columbus on 12 October 1492. It was the first landfall in the Americas and he named the island San Salvador, which means Savior, presumably expressing his feelings at having been at sea for weeks heading into the unknown. While the actual location of this island is still disputed in some quarters, most experts believe

The Lucayan Arawaks

These were a peaceful people who grew basic crops, such as maize, manioc and peppers, fished and foraged for food, with turtles and iguanas providing a plentiful source. They lived in round thatched 'hurricane proof' huts in small villages ruled by a *cacique* (chieftain), and were skilled potters, weavers and boatbuilders. Their dug out canoes were incredibly seaworthy, and their weaving skills were such that they could weave totally watertight baskets from strips of palms. The Indians also slept in beds slung between two poles, and the hammock is one of their legacies. They worshipped gods of nature, represented by statues or idols made of wood, stone or bone. Between 1492 and 1508, it is estimated that as many as 40,000 Lucayans living on the islands were carried off by the Spanish to work as slaves in the silver and gold mines on Hispaniola. Most of those who remained were killed by the Spanish or died because of their lack of resistance to diseases introduced by the conquistadores.

it was San Salvador (also called Watling Island for a time after an infamous British pirate), although some say it was either the nearby Cat Island or Samana Cay 60 miles (97km) to the south-east.

Long before the Spaniards arrived the islands were settled by Amerindians who had traveled through the Caribbean from South America. These Lucayan Arawaks (*lukku Cairi*) are thought to have arrived from the nearby Caribbean islands to the south having been displaced by the warlike Carib Indians. Their name for the island on which Columbus landed was Guanahani.

PORTUGUESE INTEREST

Following Columbus' discovery, the islands were also claimed by Portugal but in 1494, under the Treaty of Tordesillas, they were identified as Spanish although there was no attempt to settle them, largely because

there were richer pickings elsewhere, and the reef-strewn seas around The Bahamas were very treacherous and claimed scores of ships. Ponce de Leon visited in 1513 in his search for the Fountain of Youth that he thought he had found on South Bimini, but then he changed his mind and sailed off to continue his quest.

Surprisingly, the strategic importance of The Bahamas, lying as they did across the mouth of the Gulf of Mexico, and the gateway to the New World and the Caribbean, was not identified for more than 100 years, and only then were they fiercely fought over by the European colonial powers.

TROUBLED TIMES

In 1629 the English King Charles I gave The Bahamas and the Carolinas to Sir Robert Heath, his

Continued on page 12...

CLIMATE

The balmy year-round climate is one of the great attractions of The Bahamas and the reason why it has long been such a popular tourist destination. The average winter temperature is 70°F (21°C), and the average summer temperature 80°F (27°C). Temperatures rarely fall below 60°F (15°C) and seldom climb above 90°F (32°C) because of the prevailing trade winds – from the northeast during the winter, and the southeast in summer.

Average annual rainfall is about 44in (112cm), and most of the rain falls during the summer.

Grand Bahama

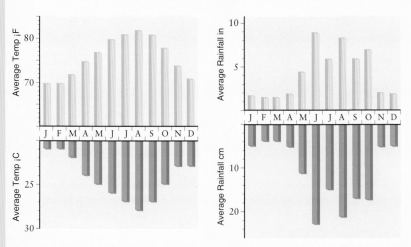

Hurricane season lasts from June to November with September and October usually the busiest months for tropical storms. The Out Islands were badly damaged by Hurricane Andrew in 1992, which was one of the worst storms of the century, but little trace can be seen today. In fact, many hotels and properties took the opportunity of making improvements and expanding. Tropical storms are well monitored, and in reality, most do not make landfall, but if a hurricane threatens, follow the advice given locally. The islands have detailed hurricane action plans designed to protect both people and property.

When to Go

Many people feel that between September and May is the best time to visit The Bahamas because it is dryer and slightly cooler. Temperatures, however, do not vary a great deal throughout the year and any time is a good time to visit.

Shopping at the International Bazaar, Freeport

attorney general, but it was not until the 1640s that a serious attempt at settlement was made. Religious intolerance in Bermuda persuaded Captain William Sayle, a former Governor of Bermuda, to seek an island where he and others could worship freely. In July 1647, the Company of Eleutherian Adventurers was formed in London, with the aim of establishing 'the Plantation of the Islands of Eleuthera, formerly called Buhama in the America, and the Adjacent Islands.' Eleuthera is the Greek word for freedom. Sayle and some 70 followers sailed in two ships for Bermuda and landed on an island called Cigatoo in the late summer of 1648. One of the ships foundered on the reefs as they neared the island. They renamed the island Eleuthera, but the group did not get on and split into two settlements.

These were, however, short lived because of squabbling, attacks by the Spanish and poor soil that made growing crops difficult. Sayle and most of the Adventurers returned to Bermuda, but they had explored the area and found the fine harbor on a nearby island that they called New Providence.

ENGLISH SETTLEMENT

In 1656, the Bermuda dissidents tried again, establishing a settlement on New Providence, but it was not until 1670 that things took off. In 1663 King Charles II of England gave South Carolina to a number of his aristocratic friends for their support against Cromwell. The new Lords Proprietors appointed Sayle as Governor, and he persuaded them to develop The Bahamas. In 1670 Charles II granted the islands to a consortium led by the Duke of Albemarle, and New Providence,

because it already had a small settlement, became the capital. In 1671 John Wentworth was appointed as first Governor, and a parliament was established.

By the early eighteenth century, it was obvious that the Lords Proprietors could not control the island, and law-abiding settlers petitioned the King to take control of The Bahamas. It was declared a crown colony in 1717 and the king leased the islands to Captain Woodes Rogers, a former privateer, and appointed him the first Royal Governor with orders to restore law and order and throw the pirates out. The new Governor arrived in The Bahamas in 1718 with a force of 1,000 troops and ordered the pirates to surrender. More than 1,000 accepted the amnesty, while those who

Piracy

The settlement on New Providence had a traumatic start, however, because the islands and their rocky cays were an ideal haven for pirates and privateers who hid there between raids on passing Spanish galleons. The Bahamas became the base for many well-known pirates including Sir Henry Morgan and Calico Jack Rackham, who sailed with Mary Read and Ann Bonny, perhaps the two most famous of all women pirates. And, there was also the infamous Captain Edward Teach from Bristol, better known as Blackbeard.

The pirates, most of them English, were unofficially tolerated because of their attacks on Spanish

refused were hunted down and hanged. The policy was so successful that the pirates chose other bases elsewhere in the Caribbean, and by 1728 the islands adopted the motto: *Expulsis piratis restituta commercia* (Pirates expelled, commerce restored), and by 1729, the islands' first assembly was convened.

Nassau, originally called Charles Towne in 1660 after Charles II, was renamed in 1689 when William and Mary came to the throne, Nassau being an historic region of Germany under William's rule. The town had to be largely rebuilt after being attacked by the Spanish and then during the Revolutionary War in 1776, a US naval task force invaded Nassau. Although the occupation lasted only a few days, it triggered a period of great unrest.

vessels and the treasures they brought back to Nassau, but the islands paid a heavy price. While the pirates could run for cover among the reefs after their raids, Nassau was an easy target for Spain seeking revenge and the town was sacked several times by the Spanish. Spain, often in alliance with France, attacked the islands many times, and on occasions, occupied them. Even when the islands were not being attacked, it was difficult to establish law and order, because many of the settlers were themselves engaged in piracy or wrecking, which was far more profitable than farming or fishing. In 1684 the English parliament passed a law banning piracy on the islands, but it had no obvious impact, and Nassau in particular, was known for its lawlessness.

In May 1782, while Britain and Spain were at war, a Spanish force attacked the colony, which surrendered. Although the islands were restored to Britain in January 1783 under the Treaty of Versailles, the Spanish were slow to leave, and in April, Colonel Andrew Devaux retook them for the English crown. The population of the islands was also boosted at the end of the American Revolution, when the English crown offered land grants to loyalists who did not want to remain in the new United States. One of these immigrants was Lord Dunmore, a former Governor of New York and Virginia, who was Governor of the colony from 1786 to 1797. The white loyalists brought their slaves with them, and in ten years, the white population of the island doubled, and the slave population had trebled.

Many of the new settlers established cotton plantations but the soil was poor and insect attack ruined the crops, and when slavery was abolished on 1 August 1834, it was no longer economic to produce. After Emancipation, however, all slaves had to agree to serve a four-year 'apprenticeship'. They had to promise to agree to working free for their former bosses for at least three-quarters of their working week. In effect, slavery was not abolished until 1838, and in 1841, the island's first legislative council was established by royal decree.

MORE RECENT TIMES

The islands prospered greatly because of their closeness to the United States both during the American Civil War when ships, loaded with

Continued on page 16...

Above: Fountain and Harbour Tower, Nassau
Below: Legislature, Nassau

Above; Left: Mount Alvernia is the highest point in The Bahamas, 206ft (63m)

Above; Right: Flamingo Pond, Garden of the Groves on Grand Bahama Island

Right: Trader in the old Straw Market, Nassau

weapons and gun powder, could make a fortune blockade running, and during Prohibition when huge quantities of alcohol passed through The Bahamas.

Following this boom period in the 1920s, attempts were made to boost fruit production for export, but these, like the sponge industry, failed in the late 1930's. After World War II, tourism became the major industry and was and continues to be, a huge success story.

Royal Governor

In 1939 after the outbreak of World War II, the Duke of Windsor, who had abdicated the British throne in 1936 in order to marry the American divorcee Mrs Wallis Simpson, escaped to Madrid from Paris after France was invaded by Germany. He offered his services to Britain but instead of being recalled to London, was immediately dispatched to The Bahamas as Governor, a position he held until 1945 when he returned to his home in Paris.

Full adult suffrage was introduced in 1962, and in May 1963, at a constitutional conference in London, The Bahamas were granted full internal self-rule. In 1969, the islands adopted the name of The Commonwealth of The Bahamas Islands, and on 10 July 1973, under the leadership of Lynden Pindling, achieved full independence, changing the name to The Commonwealth of The Bahamas. The country's new motto became: Forward, Upward, Onward Together.

THE PEOPLE

The Bahamas has a population of about 255,000 with 172,000 living on Nassau and 42,000 in Freeport. The people are a mix of European and African, with the majority of the population directly descended from slaves. Many European nationalities are represented, most originally from England, Scotland and Ireland, but also Greece. While there is still a strong British tradition on the island with cricket, afternoon tea and garden fêtes, the influence of their closeness to the United States can easily be seen, with American cars, and even an American twang in the speech. There is also a significant minority that emigrated from Haiti, which still speaks French or its Creole dialect.

Most of the population lives in urban areas, and most people are employed in tourism or related industries. New Providence Island has the largest population with almost two-thirds of all Bahamians living there in the capital Nassau, or the resorts of Cable Beach and Paradise Island. The Freeport-Lucaya area on Grand Bahama Island is the second largest populated area.

PEOPLE-TO-PEOPLE PROGRAM

This long-standing program is sponsored by the Ministry of Tourism, and offers a great way of getting to know Bahamian hospitality and culture at first hand. You can meet islanders who share the same interests, in their own homes, or at civic clubs or churches. The program matches guests with island volun-

The Abaco Islands covers 650 sq miles (1691sq km), has a population of about 10,000 and is famous as a focus of boat building and yachting. It includes Great Abaco, covering 372 sq miles (968sq km), Little Abaco, Elbow Cay, Great Guana Cay, Walker's Cay, Treasure Cay, Green Turtle Cay, Gorda Cay, Man O'War Cay and Pelican Cays.

The Andros Islands, is the largest but least explored island chain in the group covering 2,300 sq miles (5983sq km). They have a population of 8,810, are known as the bone-fishing Capital of the World, and include North Andros, Central Andros and South Andros.

The Berry Islands cover 30 small islands, scores of tiny cays, and an area of 12 sq miles (31sq km). They are a Mecca for sport fishing, and have a population of about 700.

Bimini Islands, covering 9 sq miles (23sq km) are the closest to Florida and just 50 miles (80km) off the south-east coast. The two Bimini islands, North and South, are regarded by many as the 'big game fishing capital of the world'. They have a combined population of 1,600.

Cat Island covers 150 sq miles (390sq km), has a population of 1,698, and has the highest point in The Bahamas at 206ft (63m).

Crooked Island covers 92 sq miles (239sq km), and has large areas of tidal flats and deep creeks offering excellent fishing. The population is 412.

Eleuthera covers 200 sq miles (520sq km) and includes the main island of Eleuthera, plus Cupid's Cay, Spanish Wells and Harbour Island. They have a population of about 10,600, and are noted for their fabulous pink sand beaches.

The Exuma Islands cover Great Exuma, Little Exuma and Exuma Cays, and an area of 112 sq miles (291sq km). The islands, with a population of about 4,000, are popular with yachtsmen from around the world.

Grand Bahama includes Freeport-Lucaya, The Bahamas' second largest city, and the resort area of West End. It covers 530 sq miles (1379sq km), and has a population of 50,000.

Inagua Islands, consisting of Great and Little Inagua, are the most southerly of The Bahamas islands, and cover 645 sq miles (1678sq km). They are best known as the sanctuary for 50,000 West Indian flamingos. They have a population of 985.

Long Island, with its hills and limestone caves, is fast becoming popular as a dive area. It covers 173 sq miles (450sq km), and has a population of about 2,954.

Mayaguana is an island getaway for those who can get there by boat. There are few tourist facilities and no docks, so tenders are needed to get ashore. The island covers 110 sq miles (286sq km) and has a population of 312.

New Providence Island with the capital Nassau, and resort areas of Cable Beach and Paradise Island, covers 80 sq miles (208sq km), and has a population of 172,196.

San Salvador is the island where Columbus first stepped ashore in 1492. It covers 63 sq miles (164sq km) and has a population of 465.

teers based on ages, careers, hobbies and particular interests. It is free and open to anyone who wants to participate. The People-to-People program is available on Grand Bahama, Abaco, Bimini, Eleuthera, Exuma and San Salvador. For more details call: 242-356-0435 (Nassau), 242-352-8044 (Freeport/Lucaya), or contact any Bahamas Tourist Office.

Ideally, try to register for the program at least three weeks before arriving on the island to allow a match of your first choice interests to be arranged. Every effort will still be made to find a match, however, even if you cannot register before arriving on the islands. One of the program's highlights is the tea party held at Government House on the last Friday of each month between January and August.

CULTURE

The culture of the islands reflects the backgrounds of its people, and those from nearby islands. The main festival is the **Junkanoo Parade** in Nassau that takes place on Boxing Day and New Year's Day, attracting thousands of costumed dancers, bands, drums and pulsating African rhythms. On both days, the parades start at around 3am as the groups assemble in different parts of town. Junkanoo is a cross between Caribbean carnival, Mardi Gras, and the traditional Mummer's Parade and incorporates many ancient African tribal rituals in song and dance. The revelers, dressed in wonderful, vivid creations march and dance to the sounds of goatskin drums, cowbells, whistles and other home made instruments, and compete for prizes for the best costumes.

The costumes are usually different on both days, and parades are held in Freeport, Grand Bahama and the Family Islands.

The other main festival is **Goombay** that has taken place at various places over the summer, with parades, fairs and cultural events. Goombay, the Bantu word for rhythm, is also the traditional music of the Bahamas, blending the musical traditions of Africa and Europe. The islands' African tradition is still represented in Bahamian folklore with legends of demons, magic and strange benevolent monsters, such as the Chickcharnies.

Nassau has a very professional repertory company that performs drama, dance and musicals, at the Dundas Centre for the Performing Arts. There are numerous galleries exhibiting the work of talented local artists, and many other drama and dance groups.

There is a permanent exhibition of the paintings of Amos Ferguson at the Pompey Museum. The works of Ferguson have been declared a national treasure, and his 'primitive' paintings are grouped under four main themes – history, religion, nature and folklore. Other artists to have achieved international acclaim are Maxwell Taylor and Stan Burnside.

Of special note are the active Historical Society that works to preserve the Bahamians' tradition and local history; the National Trust that was founded in 1959, and works to preserve old buildings and wildlife, and the Department of Archives which has a fascinating collection of old records and photographs which are available for viewing.

216

Junkanoo Parade

THE ECONOMY

Tourism is the major industry of the islands, which have few natural resources. Many of the resort complexes and hotels are foreign-owned, or have been built in conjunction with foreign investors, and the continued popularity of the islands with cruise ships and its popularity as a holiday destination for North Americans, means that there is a much higher than average standard of living for the islanders. The islands attract about three million tourists a year, about half of them arriving aboard cruise ships.

Farming and fishing, especially for crawfish, are traditional occupations pursued by the same families for many generations, especially in the southernmost islands. During the mid-1800s a sponge industry was established, together with pineapple and sisal plantations. Sponges were harvested until the late 1930s but it is now more of a tourist attraction.

Banking and finance is now the second largest industry and The Bahamas continues to grow as a major international finance area. Other industries include food and fish processing, pharmaceuticals, a petrochemicals refinery, and salt production from solar-powered desalination plants. A hard limestone called aragonite, which is used in the production of a number of products from cement and steel, to glass and petrochemicals, is quarried at Sandy Cay. Exports include salt, frozen crawfish, vegetables, citrus, rum and aragonite.

Because of its maritime laws, merchant shipping from any nationality can fly under the Bahamian flag, so The Bahamas merchant marine is one of the largest in the world.

THE GOVERNMENT AND JUDICIARY

The Commonwealth of The Bahamas became an independent state within the British Commonwealth on 10 July 1973. The Queen, as head of the Commonwealth and titular head of state, appoints the Governor-General, who in turn appoints the Prime Minister, who is usually the leader of the majority party in parliament. The government is based on that of the UK with an elected House of Representatives, and a Senate appointed by the Governor-General, on the advice of the Prime Minister. Members of the House of Representatives are elected every five years. The Bahamas is divided into 20 local government districts. The judiciary is also based on the UK model with magistrates' court at local level, with an Appeal Court and the ultimate authority vested in the Supreme Court.

PLANT AND ANIMAL LIFE

Along the roads, you can spot giant ferns and massive stands of towering bamboo, bananas, coconut groves, hanging breadfruit, mango and pawpaw, and the most stunning array of spectacularly bright flowering plants from giant African tulip trees festooned with scarlet blossom to tiny orchids. Bougainvillea flowers everywhere, there are scores of varieties of hibiscus, frangipani and poinsettia. There are heliconia, also known as the lobster plant, bird of paradise flowers and poinciana everywhere. The flamboyant tree is also known as the tourist tree because it bursts into bloom during the summer and is a blaze of vivid shades.

Originally the islands were covered by forest, mostly of Caribbean pine, wild guava and thatch palm, and there are still areas of hardwoods and pine forests, and in areas of lower rainfall, the vegetation consists of thorn, cactus, yucca, mesquite and scrub woodland. Along the coast you can find swamps, mangroves and marsh woodlands. Generally, however, the vegetation consists of shrubs and low trees.

Dangerous tree

Note: The manchineel, which can be found on many beaches, has a number of effective defensive mechanisms that can prove very painful. Trees vary from a few feet to more than 30ft in height, and have widely spreading, deep forked boughs with small, dark green leaves and yellow stems, and fruit like small, green apples. If you examine the leaves carefully without touching them, you will notice a small pinhead- sized raised dot at the junction of leaf and leaf stalk. The apple-like fruit is poisonous, and sap from the tree causes very painful blisters. It is so toxic, that early Caribs are said to have dipped their arrowheads in it before hunting trips. Sap is released if a leaf or branch is broken, and more so after rain. Avoid contact with the tree, don't sit under it, or on a fallen branch, and do not eat the fruit. If you do get sap on your skin, run into the sea and wash it off as quickly as possible.

Beach morning glory with its array of pink flowers is found on many beaches, and is important because its roots help prevent sand drift. The plant also produces nectar, from glands in the base of its leaf stalks, that attracts ants, and it is thought this evolution has occurred so that the ants will discourage any leaf-nibbling predators. Other beach plants include seagrape and the manchineel, which should be treated with caution.

Of course, the sea teems with bright vivid fish and often, even more spectacular is the coral and marine plants. Even if you just float upside down in the water with a facemask on, you will be able to enjoy many of the beautiful underwater scenes, but the best way to see things is by scuba diving, snorkeling or taking a trip in a glass-bottomed boat.

There are hard and soft corals and only one – the fire coral – poses a threat to swimmers and divers, because if touched, it causes a stinging skin rash. Among the more spectacular corals are deadman's fingers, staghorn, brain coral and seafans, and there are huge sea anemones and sponges, while tropical fish species include the parrotfish, blue tang surgeonfish, tiny but aggressive damselfish, angelfish and brightly shaded wrasse. Whales and dolphins can also be seen offshore.

Coastal swamps also provide a rich habitat for wildlife. Tiny tree crabs and burrowing edible land crabs scurry around in the mud trapped in the roots of mangrove trees just above water level. Herons, egrets, pelicans and often frigate birds roost in the higher branches,

Continued on page 24...

Abaco

Abaco National Park: The 20,500 acre (8,200 hectare) park in south eastern Great Abaco, was established in 1994 and includes 5,000 acres (2,000 hectares) of forest, the major habitat of the endangered Bahama parrot.

Black Sound Cay Reserve: This small 1.5-acre park off Green Turtle Cay includes mangrove vegetation, a habitat rich in water fowl and winter migratory birds.

Tilloo Cay: The 11 acre (4.5 hectares) reserve just north of Tilloo Pond, includes the nesting grounds of a number of tropical birds, and is an important refuge for a number of species of migratory bird in passage.

Conception Island

Conception Island National Park: This is an important refuge for many of the island's sea birds, birds on migration and green turtles. It also has historical significance as one of the three Bahamian islands on which Columbus is known to have landed.

Exuma

Exuma Cays Land and Sea Park: A 176 sq mile (458sq km) park created in 1958, and the first of its kind in the world. It was the first marine fishery reserve in the Caribbean, and is noted for its outstanding unspoiled beauty.

Grand Bahama

Lucayan National Park: The 40-acre (16 hectare) a quarter of a mile to the east of Freeport, includes the longest known underwater cave and cavern system in the world, with over 6 miles (10km) of caves and tunnels so far charted. Above ground, every type of vegetation zone found in The Bahamas can be found.

Left: Lucayan National Park

Opposite page;
Top: Abaco Parrot, only found in The Bahamas
Middle: A native Iguana
Bottom: Flamingos, the national bird of The Bahamas

Peterson Cay National Park: The 1.5-acre (0.6 hectare) park includes the only cave on Grand Bahama's leeward shore. It is an area of outstanding natural beauty, and very popular with the islanders over the weekend.

The Rand Nature Centre: The 100 acre (40 hectare) reserve in the heart of downtown Freeport was acquired by The Bahamas National Trust in 1992. It has a flock of resident West Indian flamingos, a delightful nature trail that winds through natural coppice and pines, and the administrative office of The Bahamas National Trust on Grand Bahama.

Great Abaco

Pelican Cays Land and Sea Park: The 2,100 acre (840 hectares) park is 8 miles (13km) north of Cherokee Sound, and is famous for its underwater caves, coral reefs and rich marine life, and land flora and fauna.

Great Inagua

Inagua National Park: the world's largest breeding colony of West Indian flamingos. The park covers 287 sq miles (747sq km).

Union Creek Reserve: A 7 sq mile (18sq km) area of enclosed tidal creek, and an important site for sea turtle research, especially the Green turtle.

New Providence

The Retreat: This 11 acre (4.4 hectare) botanic garden in Nassau contains one of the largest private collections of palms in the world, and also houses the administrative headquarters of The Bahamas National Trust.

Importance of coral

There are scores of different multi-shaded corals that make up the reefs offshore. These extensive reefs account for about five per cent of all the coral in the world, and few people appreciate just what an important resource coral is. Coral, like the tropical rain forests, is essential in helping regulate the earth's atmosphere, by acting as a 'carbon sink'. Both coral and the trees in the rain forests are able to absorb carbon dioxide from the atmosphere. If coral reefs are destroyed and tropical rain forests felled, carbon dioxide levels increase resulting in the 'greenhouse effect' and the threat of global warming. Ironically, if temperatures were to rise globally by just a few degrees, the polar ice caps would thaw faster, ocean levels would rise, and most of the low-lying islands of The Bahamas would be submerged. Water temperatures would also kill the remaining coral and have a devastating effect on marine life.

while the mangrove cuckoo shares the lower branches with belted kingfishers.

Gardens are often filled with bright flowers in bloom year round, growing alongside exotic vegetables like yam, sweet potato, and dasheen. A wide variety of fruit trees can be seen with extensive citrus groves, avocado, sweetsop, soursop, papaya and bananas are grown almost everywhere.

The flowers attract hummingbirds like the doctor bird, as well as the carib grackle, a strutting, starling-like bird with a paddle-shaped tail, and friendly bananaquit. You can also spot tree lizards, and the larger geckos that hunt at night.

Along roadsides and hedgerows in the countryside, you can see the vine-like caralita, calabash with its gourd-like fruits, tamarind and distinctive star-shaped leaves of the castor bean, whose seeds when crushed yield castor oil.

Areas of scrubland have their own flora or fauna, with plants bursting into color following the first heavy rains after the dry season. There are century plants, with their prickly, sword like leaves, which grow for up to twenty years before flowering. The yellow flower stalk grows at a tremendous rate for several days and can reach 20ft high, but having bloomed once the whole plant then dies. Other typical scrubland vegetation includes aloe, acacia, prickly pear and several species of cactus.

There are hundreds of species of insects, several species of frogs and a number of different bats, which live in caves along the rocky coast. There are also several species of snake, including the Bahamian boa constrictor that locally is called the fowl snake, but all are non-poisonous. The largest animals are all domesticated, and mainly cattle, sheep and horses.

The warm waters attract manatee, or sea cow, the animals which early mariners thought were mermaids – obviously after having been at sea for too long, or having drunk too much local rum.

Larger animals

There are few large wild animals other than some wild boar and a few wild donkeys in remote areas, but you can see agouti, a reddish-brown rodent which can grow up to 24in (60cm) long, and the small tree-living hutia, both considered delicacies by some islanders. There are also wild cats in the Abaco forests, raccoons that were imported to the islands to destroy rats in the sugar cane plantations, the endangered Bahamian rock iguana and many species of smaller lizard. There is the Cat Island Terrapin, and several species of turtle, including Hawksbill, can be seen.

BIRD LIFE

The islands teem with bird life, including the Bahamian (or Cuban) parrot, which now numbers about 3,000, although it is still on the endangered list. It is found on Inagua and Abaco, but the parrots on each have developed very different nesting habits. The parrots on Inagua generally nest in holes in trees, while those on Abaco nest in cracks in the rocky limestone ground – the only ground nesting parrots in the New World – but this does make them more vulnerable to predators, especially wild cats found in the Abaco forests. The Abaco National Park covering 20,000 acres (8,000 hectares) was specially created to take in the nesting area and habitat of this rare bird.

The graceful pink flamingo is the national bird, and The Bahamas has the world's largest nesting colony of West Indian flamingos. In 1956 there were fewer than 5,000 flamingos, but a very successful conservation and breeding schedule has seen the number swell to more than 60,000. The main colony is at Inagua, but the flamingoes can be seen at other feeding grounds, especially on Crooked Island and Andros.

Offshore you may see the magnificent frigate bird, easily recognizable by its size, long black seven-foot wingspan, forked tail and apparent effortless ability to glide on the winds. There are brown booby birds, named by sailors from the Spanish word for 'fool' because they were so easy to catch. Pelicans that look so ungainly on land yet are so acrobatic in the air, are common, as are laughing gulls and royal terns. Several species of sandpiper can usually be seen scurrying around at the water's edge. Other indigenous species include white crowned pigeon, gray catbird, mocking bird or thrasher, red legged thrush, the tiny blue gray grantcatcher, black and white warbler, greater American pewee, tanagers, Bahama woodstar and emerald hummingbirds and belted kingfisher.

If you are really interested in bird watching, pack a small pair of binoculars. The new mini-binoculars are ideal for island bird watching, because the light is normally so good

Continued on page 28...

Cruise Ship in dock

that you will get a clear image despite the small object lens.

On Grand Bahama bird watching walks take place at 7am during the summer and 8am in the winter on the first Saturday of the month. For more details, calls ☎ 352-5438. The best birding on New Providence is in the western half of the island.

EDIBLE PLANTS

As most of the plants, fruits, vegetables and spices will be new to the first time visitor, the following brief descriptions are offered. All either grow on the islands, or are sold in the markets and may be used in island dishes:

Bananas

Bananas are one of the Caribbean's most important exports, hence their nickname 'green gold' – and they grow everywhere. There are three types of banana plant. The most common is the banana that we normally buy in supermarkets. It originated in Malaya and was introduced into the Caribbean in the early sixteenth century by the Spanish. The large green bananas, or plantains, originally came from southern India, and are used mainly in cooking. They are often fried and served as an accompaniment to fish and meat. The third variety is the red banana, which is not grown commercially, but which can occasionally be seen around the islands.

Most banana plantations cover only a few acres and are worked by the owner or tenant, although there are still some large holdings. A banana produces a crop about every nine months, and each cluster of flowers grows into a hand of bananas. A bunch can contain up to twenty hands of bananas, with each hand having up to 20 individual fruit.

Although they grow tall, bananas are not trees but herbaceous plants which die back each year. Once the plant has produced fruit, a shoot from the ground is cultivated to take its place, and the old plant dies. Bananas need a lot of attention, and island farmers will tell you that there are not enough hours in a day to do everything that needs to be done. The crop needs fertilizing regularly, leaves need cutting back, and you will often see the fruit inside blue tinted plastic containers, which protect it from insect and bird attack, and speed up maturation.

Breadfruit

Breadfruit were brought to the Caribbean by the infamous Captain Bligh in 1793. He brought 1200 breadfruit saplings from Tahiti aboard the Providence, and these were first planted in Jamaica and

Mutiny on the Bounty

It was Bligh's attempts to bring in young breadfruit trees that led to the mutiny on the *Bounty* four years earlier. Bligh was given the command of the 215-ton *Bounty* in 1787 and was ordered to take the breadfruit trees from Tahiti to the West Indies where they were to be used to provide cheap food for the slaves. The ship had collected its cargo and had reached Tonga when the crew under Fletcher Christian mutinied. The crew claimed that Bligh's regime was too tyrannical, and he and 18 members of the crew

St. Vincent, and then quickly spread throughout the islands.

Whatever the reason for the mutiny, the breadfruit is a cheap carbohydrate-rich food, although pretty tasteless when boiled. It is best eaten fried, baked or roasted over charcoal. The slaves did not like them at first, but the tree spread and can now be found almost everywhere. It has large, dark green leaves, and the large green fruits can weigh 10-12lbs (about 5k). The falling fruits explode with a loud bang and splatter its pulpy contents over a large distance. It is said that no one goes hungry when the breadfruit is in season.

Calabash

Calabash trees are native to the Caribbean and have huge gourd like fruits that are very versatile when dried and cleaned. They can be used as water containers and bowls, bailers for boats, and as lanterns.

---

who stayed loyal to him, were cast adrift in an open boat. The cargo of breadfruit was dumped overboard.

Bligh, in a remarkable feat of seamanship, navigated the boat for 3,600 miles until making landfall on Timor in the East Indies. Some authorities have claimed that it was the breadfruit tree cargo that sparked the mutiny, as each morning the hundreds of trees in their heavy containers had to be carried on deck, and then carried down into the hold at nightfall. It might have proved just too much for the already overworked crew.

Juice from the pulp is boiled into thick syrup and used to treat coughs and colds, and the fruit is said to have many other medicinal uses.

Cocoa

Cocoa is another important crop, and its Latin name *theobroma* means 'food of the gods'. A cocoa tree can produce several thousand flowers a year, but only a fraction of these will develop into seed bearing pods. It is the heavy orange pods that hang from the cocoa tree which contain the beans that contain the seeds that produce cocoa and chocolate. The beans, containing a sweet, white sap that protects the seeds, are split open and kept in trays to ferment. This process takes up to eight days and the seeds must be kept at a regular temperature to ensure the right taste and aroma develops. The seeds are then dried. In the old days people used to walk barefoot over the beans to polish them to enhance their appearance. Today, the beans are crushed to extract cocoa butter, and the remaining powder is cocoa. Chocolate is made by mixing cocoa powder, cocoa butter and sugar.

Coconut

Coconut palms are everywhere and should be treated with caution. Anyone who has heard the whoosh of a falling coconut knows how scary the sound is. Those who did not hear the sound presumably did not live to tell the tale. Actually, very few people get injured in this way and that is a near miracle in view of the tens of thousands of palms all over the island, but it is not a good idea to picnic in a coconut grove!

Coconut trees are incredibly hardy, able to grow in sand and even when regularly washed by salty sea-

Above; Left: Cat Island Right: UNEXSO, Grand Bahama
Below: Port Lucaya Market Place

water. They can also survive long periods without rain. Their huge leaves, up to 20ft long in mature trees, drop down during dry spells so that a smaller surface area is exposed to the sun, reducing evaporation. Coconut palms can grow up to 80ft tall, and produce up to 100 seeds a year. The seeds are the second largest in the plant kingdom, and these fall when ripe.

The coconut traditionally bought in greengrocers, is a giant seed. The white edible 'meat' is enclosed by a hard shell of fibrous copra and this is covered by a large green husk. The seed and protective coverings can weigh 30lb and more. The seed and casing is waterproof, drought proof and able to float, and this explains why coconut palms, which originated in the Pacific and Indian Oceans, are now found throughout the Caribbean – the seeds literally floated across the seas.

Coconut palms have many uses. The leaves can be used as thatch for roofing, or cut into strips and woven into mat and baskets, while the husks yield coir, a fiber resistant to salt water and ideal for ropes and brushes and brooms. Green coconuts contain delicious thirst-quenching 'milk', and the coconut 'meat' can be eaten raw, or baked in ovens for two days before being sent to processing plants where the oil is extracted. Coconut oil is used in cooking, soaps, and synthetic rubber and even in hydraulic brake fluid.

As you drive around the island, you will see groups of men and women splitting the coconuts in half with machetes preparing them for the ovens. You might also see halved coconut shells spaced out on the corrugated tin roofs of some homes. These are being dried before being sold to the copra processing plants.

Dasheen

Dasheen is one of the crops known as 'ground provisions' in the Caribbean, the others being sweet potatoes, yams, eddy and tannia. The last two are close relatives of dasheen, and all are members of the aroid family, some of the world's oldest cultivated crops. Dasheen with its 'elephant ear' leaves, and eddo grow from a corm which when boiled thoroughly can be used like potato, and the young leaves of either are used to make calaloo, a spinach-like soup. Both dasheen and eddo are thought to have come from China or Japan but tannia is native to the Caribbean, and its roots can be boiled, baked or fried. It grows wild in The Bahamas but is not generally used for food.

Guava

Guava is common throughout the West Indies, and the aromatic, pulpy fruit is also a preferred choice with birds who then distribute its seeds. The fruit-bearing shrub can be seen on roadsides and in gardens, and it is used to make a wide range of products from jelly to 'cheese', a paste made by mixing the fruit with sugar. The fruit ranges from a golf ball to a tennis ball in size, and is a rich source of vitamin A with lots more vitamin C than citrus fruit.

Mango

Mango can be delicious if somewhat messy to eat. It originally came from India but is now grown throughout the Caribbean and found wherever there are people. Young mangoes can be stringy and unappetizing, but ripe fruit from mature trees that grow up to 50ft and more, are usually delicious, and can be eaten raw or cooked. The juice is a great reviver in the morning, and the fruit is often used to make jams and other preserves. The wood of the mango is often used by boatbuilders.

Nutmeg

Nutmeg trees are found on all the Caribbean islands but are rare in the wild on The Bahamas. The tree thrives in hilly, wet areas and the fruit is the size of a small tomato. The outer husk, which splits open while still on the tree, is used to make the very popular nutmeg jelly. Inside the seed is protected by a bright red casing that when dried and crushed, produces the spice, mace. Finally, the dark outer shell of the seed is broken open to reveal the nutmeg which is dried and then ground into a powder, or sold whole so that it can be grated to add taste to dishes.

Passion fruit

Passion fruit is not widely grown but it can usually be bought at the market. The pulpy fruit contains hundreds of tiny seeds, and many people prefer to press the fruit and drink the juice. It is also commonly used in fruit salads, sherbets and ice creams.

Pawpaw or papaya trees

Pawpaw or papaya trees are also found throughout the island and are commonly grown in gardens. The trees are prolific fruit producers but grow so quickly that the fruit soon becomes difficult to gather. The large, juicy melon-like fruits are eaten fresh, pulped for juice or used locally to make jams, preserves and ice cream. They are rich sources of vitamin A and C. The leaves and fruit contain an enzyme which tenderizes meat, and tough joints cooked wrapped in pawpaw leaves or covered in slices of fruit, usually taste like much more expensive cuts. The same enzyme, papain, is also used in chewing gum, cosmetics, the tanning industry and, somehow, in making wool shrink resistant. A tea made from unripe fruit is said to be good for lowering high blood pressure.

Pigeon Peas

Pigeon Peas are widely cultivated and can be found in many back gardens. The plants are very hardy and drought resistant, and give prolific yields of peas that can be eaten fresh or dried and used in soups and stews.

Pineapples

Pineapples were certainly grown in the Caribbean by the time Columbus arrived, and were probably brought from South America by the Amerindians. The fruit is slightly smaller than the Pacific pineapple, but the taste is more intense.

Sugar Cane

Sugar Cane is not grown commercially but can sometimes be seen growing in the wild. The cane was grown to produce molasses for the rum industry. The canes can grow up to 12ft tall and after cutting, the canes had to be crushed to extract the sugary juice. After extraction, the juice was boiled until the sugar crystallized. The mixture remaining was molasses and this was used to produce rum.

Sugar Apple

Sugar Apple is a member of the annona fruit family, and grows wild and in gardens throughout the islands. The small, soft sugar apple fruit can be peeled off in strips when ripe, and is like eating thick applesauce. They are eaten fresh or used to make sherbet or drinks. Soursop is a member of the same family, and its spiny fruits can be seen in hedgerows and gardens. They are eaten fresh or used for preserves, drinks and ice cream.

FOOD

The Bahamas offers a huge choice when it comes to eating out, from excellent traditional island fare to the finest international cuisine at the best tourist hotels. Dining out offers the chance to experiment with all sorts of unusual spices, vegetables and fruits, with Creole and island dishes, and, of course, rum punches and other exotic cocktails.

Eating out is very relaxed and most restaurants do not have a strict dress code, although most people like to wear something a little smarter at dinner after a day on the beach or out sightseeing. Many hotels have a tendency to offer buffet dinners or barbecues, but these can be interesting and tasty affairs.

BREAKFAST

Breakfast can be one of the most exciting meals of the day for a visitor. There is a huge range of fruit juices to choose from. Try a glass of

Continued on page 36...

SOME POPULAR BAHAMIAN RECIPES

Peas 'n Rice

- 2oz pork fat
- 1oz oil
- 2oz celery
- 2oz onion
- 2oz green pepper
- 4oz tomato paste
- 12oz pigeon peas (or use canned kidney beans)
- 2 pints water
- 1lb rice
- salt, pepper and thyme.

Cut the pork and vegetables into $\frac{1}{4}$ inch cubes. Fry the pork in the oil until brown then add the vegetables and cook for 3 minutes. Add the tomato paste, peas, thyme, water and season to taste. Bring to the boil and add the rice. Cover and cook for about 20 minutes.

Johnny Cake

- 2lb flour
- 2oz baking powder
- 4oz sugar
- $\frac{1}{2}$ oz salt
- 4 eggs
- 4oz butter
- nutmeg
- water

Sift the dry ingredients and then rub the butter into the flour. Add the eggs and enough water to make a firm dough. Knead well and allow to rest for at least 30 minutes. Then gently roll to a height of about two inches and bake in a moderate over for about 35 minutes.

Curry Plantain Soup

- $\frac{1}{2}$oz of diced onions or shallots
- 10 stalks of diced celery
- 2 crushed cloves of garlic
- 1oz of vegetable oil
- 1 tbs of sugar
- 1 tbs of cider vinegar
- 2 tbs of curry powder
- 6 peeled and diced plaintains
- 2 pints chicken stock
- 2 fl oz heavy cream
- 5 tsp of chopped cilantro
- salt and pepper

Heat the oil in a large pan. Add shallots, celery and garlic and sauté until golden. Stir in sugar and caramelize slightly. Add curry powder and plantains and mix well, then add chicken stock and bring mixture to the boil before allowing to simmer for 20 minutes. Add the cream and simmer for a further 10 minutes. Remove from heat and blend the soup until the texture is smooth. Sprinkle with chopped cilantro and season to taste.

watermelon juice, followed by a fresh grapefruit, or slices of chilled paw-paw or mango. Most hotels offer fruit plates offering a wide choice so you should be able to taste your way through them all during your stay.

The island's fruits also make great jams and preserves, and you can follow the fruit with piping hot toast spread with perhaps citrus marmalade or guava jam, maybe washed down with the island's own coffee. Most tourist hotels also offer traditional American breakfasts for those who cannot do without them. During the summer, there are fruits such as the guinep, plumrose, sugar apple and yellow plum.

DINNER

There is usually a good choice when it comes to dinner. Starters include a huge choice of fruit juices from orange and grapefruit to the more unusual ones like soursop and tamarind. You can also drink green coconut 'milk'.

Traditional Caribbean starters include dishes such as Christophene and coconut soup, and bean soup. Calaloo is also sometimes offered. The spinach-like soup is made throughout the Caribbean and ochroes, smoked meat and sometimes crab are added, as well as lots of herbs and spices. Chicken nuggets and marinated green bananas are also popular starters.

Fish and clam chowders are also popular starters. Try heart of palm, excellent fresh shrimps or scallops, smoked kingfish wrapped in crêpes or crab backs, succulent land crab meat sautéed with breadcrumbs and seasoning, and served stuffed in the shell. It is much sweeter than the meat of sea crabs.

The fish is generally excellent, and don't be alarmed if you see dolphin on the menu. It is not the protected species made famous by 'Flipper', but a solid, close-textured flat-faced fish called the dorado, which is delicious. Salt fish often appears on the menu. Salting was the most common form of food preserving, and allowed surplus catches to be safely kept until times of food shortage, or for when the seas were too rough for the fishing boats to go to sea.

There is also snapper, grouper, kingfish, redfish, jacks, balaouy, snapper, tuna, flying fish, lobster, swordfish, baby squid and mussels.

Try conch chowder or seafood jambalaya, chunks of lobster, shrimps and ham served on a bed of braised seasoned rice, shrimp Creole, with fresh shrimp sautéed in garlic butter and parsley and served with tomatoes, or fish Creole, with fresh fish steaks cooked in a spicy onion, garlic and tomato sauce and served with rice and fried plantain.

Conch (pronounced 'konk') is almost the national dish and is served in scores of different ways from chowders and soups, to salads and fritters. Another specialty is Bahamian Stew Fish, a dish of celery, onions, tomatoes, spices and fish. The spiny Bahamian rock lobster is excellent.

There is delicious spicy chicken, and you can try souse, a stew containing vegetables and anything else the cook wants to add, often pig's trotters. Other regularly served dishes are Peas 'n Rice, a dish made from pigeon peas, salt pork, tomatoes, celery, rice, peppers and thyme; and Johnny Cake, which is pan cooked bread made from flour, butter, milk, sugar, salt and baking powder, and delicious when served hot.

For vegetarians there are excellent salads, and you might find stuffed breadfruit, callaloo bake, stuffed squash and pawpaw, baked sweet potato and yam casserole that are traditional Caribbean dishes not commonly served in hotels and restaurants.

On the buffet table, you might also see a dish called pepper pot. This is usually hot and spicy meat and vegetable stew to which may be added small flour dumplings and shrimps.

There are wonderful breads, and you should try them if you get the chance. There are banana and pumpkin breads, and delicious cakes such as coconut loaf cake, guava jelly cookies and rum cake.

For dessert, try fresh fruit salad, with added cherry juice, and sometimes a little rum, which is a year round popular dessert. There are a wide variety of fruit sherbets using tropical fruits such as banana, coconut, soursop, mango, sappodilla, gooseberry, pineapple and tamarind.

Or, try one of the exotically tasting ice creams. There are also banana fritters and banana flambé, coconut cheesecake, green papaya or guava shells simmered in heavy syrup. Guava Duff is a special Bahamian dessert.

DRINKS

Columbus is credited with planting the first sugar cane in the Caribbean, on Hispaniola, during his third voyage, and the Spanish called it *aguardiente de cana*, meaning cane liquor. The Latin name for sugar cane is *saccharum*, and it was English sailors who shortened this to rum. A more lively suggestion is that the name comes from the old English word tr*umbullion*, which means a drunken brawl.

The rum trade on The Bahamas got a major boost during the 1920s because of the Prohibition in the United States. Rum distilled on the island was smuggled into the US and this trade continued long after the end of Prohibition.

Rum is still the Caribbean drink. There are almost as many rums in the West Indies as there are malt whiskies in Scotland, and there is an amazing variety of strength, shade and quality. The finest rums are best drunk on the rocks, but if you want to capture a bit of the Caribbean

Beware!

Another note of warning: on most tables you will find a bottle of pepper sauce. It usually contains a blend of several types of hot pepper, spices and vinegar, and should be treated cautiously. Try a little first before splashing it all over your food, as these sauces range from hot to unbearable.

If you want to make your own hot pepper sauce, take four ripe hot peppers, one teaspoon each of oil, ketchup and vinegar and a pinch of salt, blend together into a liquid, and bottle.

Continued on page 40...

37

Above: Columbus Government House

Right: Young Bahamian

COLUMBUS
1492.

Above: Relaxing on Cat Island
Below: Port Lucaya, Grand Bahama

History of rum

The first rum on The Bahamas was produced at least 350 years ago and became an important international commodity. It figured prominently in the infamous Triangle Trade in which slaves from Africa were sold for rum from the West Indies that was sold to raise money to buy more slaves. Rum had such fortifying powers that General George Washington insisted every soldier be given a daily ration, and a daily tot also became a tradition in the British Royal Navy. The very strong Navy Rum was issued as a daily tot until 1970.

spirit, have a couple of rum punches.

Bacardi is the largest producer of rum, and some of its aged rums are considered among the world's finest. The distillery on New Providence is open for tours and tasting. There is the fine TodHunter distillery on Grand Bahama Island but it is not open to the public.

All sorts of rums are produced from light to dark and of varying strengths. Rum is aged in American white oak barrels, and the longer it remains in the barrel, the more taste it will absorb. Traditionally, dark rum spent a long time ageing in barrels, and light rums only a short time. Today, most white and light rums are not aged in wood, but in stainless steel vats.

The Bahamas boasts several special 'island' blends such as Nassau Royale liqueur, Nassau Sunstroke, Coco Loco and a concoction known as Miss Emily's Goombay Smash. There are also rums tasting of coconut, banana, lemon or pineapple. Old Nassau Rums are made by Burns House in Nassau and are only available in the Bahamas, and both TodHunter and Bacardi produce excellent old rums.

RUM RECIPES

Plantation Rum Punch

To make Plantation Rum Punch, thoroughly mix 3 ounces of rum, with one ounce of limejuice and one teaspoon of honey, then pour over crushed ice, and for a little zest, add a pinch of freshly grated nutmeg.

Bahama Mama

Mix 1oz each of coconut rum, white rum and lemon juice, 2oz each of unsweetened pineapple juice and unsweetened orange juice, and half an ounce of grenadine. Shake well and pour over ice into a tall glass and serve with a slice of orange and a cherry.

Shark Bite

Mix half an ounce each of pineapple rum, gold rum, triple sec and

Amaretto, add 3 ounces of pineapple juice and 1oz of grenadine. Shake well with ice and strain into a tall glass and decorate with a cherry and wedge of fresh pineapple.

Grand Bahama Smile

Mix one and a quarter ounces of coconut rum, one sixteenth of an ounce of grenadine and 4oz of pineapple juice, shake with crushed ice.

Other Bahamian rum cocktails have exotic names such as Yellow Bird and Goombay Smash.

Most tourist hotels and bars also offer a wide range of other cocktails both alcoholic, usually very strong, and non-alcoholic. The island beer is Kalik, which is brewed on Nassau, but a huge variety of imported beers is available. Kalik (pronounced car-lik and said quickly so it almost sounds like click) gets its name from the sound made by Junkanoo cowbells.

Tap water is safe to drink and mineral and bottled water is widely available, and so are soft drinks.

Note: While many of the main tourist hotel restaurants offer excellent service, time does not have the same urgency as it does back home, and why should it after all, as you are on holiday. Relax, enjoy a drink, the company and the surroundings and don't worry if things take longer, the wait is generally worth it.

NASSAU AND NEW PROVIDENCE ISLAND

New Providence Island with the capital Nassau, and resort areas of Cable Beach and Paradise Island, is just over 20 miles (32km) long, 7 miles (11km) wide, covers 80 sq miles (208 sq km), and has a population of 172,196, the majority of whom live in or close to Nassau.

TRANSPORT ON THE ISLAND

The best way to meet the locals is to hop on a jitney, one of the mini-buses that go all over the island for a nominal fee during daylight hours. Adult fares are 75c, and 50c for children, and buses usually run every half hour. You need the exact fare as drivers cannot give change. Buses to the Cable Beach area leave from the Navy Lion Road North depot, buses to the eastern part of the island leave from Frederick Street North depot, and buses to the shopping malls leave from Marlborough Street East. Just make sure before boarding that the mini bus is going in your direction.

There are regular ferries and water taxis from Nassau across the harbor to Paradise Island, and mini-buses on Paradise Island. The ferries run every 20 minutes or so between 8am and 6pm and the fare costs $2 each way.

Taxis are readily available and charges fares fixed by the Government, but always check on what it will cost as a precaution before setting off. Approximate fares are: airport to Cable Beach $12, airport to Paradise Island $22 + $2 toll, airport to downtown $18. You can negotiate a price if you want to hire a taxi for longer trips and sight-seeing. Expect to pay around $20-25 an hour, which is a good deal if there are a number of you to share the fare, but always negotiate to see if you can get a better price

Horse drawn carriages offer a more relaxed way of touring Nassau, and the horses wearing their own straw hats know all the right places to visit. They are available from their own covered rank on Prince George Dock and rides last about 45 minutes and cost about $10 for 2.

NASSAU

The capital of The Bahamas lies on the northern edge of New Providence Island, close to the resort areas of Cable Beach and Paradise Island with their lovely beaches, luxury hotels and quaint inns, wide range of shopping, casinos, fine dining and other attractions. Apart from sun bathing, shopping and gambling you can bird watch or parachute, go deep sea fishing, scuba diving or snorkeling; there is wind surfing, yachting and power boat cruising, or you can experience the Atlantis Adventure and the Dolphin Experience.

GETTING AROUND — GRAND BAHAMA, NEW PROVIDENCE AND PARADISE ISLAND

Roads

Most of the inhabited islands of The Bahamas have good paved main roads, although some of the places of interest are along passable dirt roads. Car, jeep, scooter and bike hire is available on all the islands.

Boat

Travel between the islands is by a fleet of small boats that carry passengers, mail and cargo. The weekly mail boats sail from Potter's Cay, Nassau and visit most of the Out Islands. Get there early if you want to get on board, as this is on a first come, first served basis. It is a very affordable and interesting way to see the islands. Many hotels and resorts have their own water taxis to pick up guests, and you can always try and thumb a lift at one of the marinas if a yacht is sailing your way. There is a high-speed daily ferry link between Nassau, Harbour Island and North Eleuthera.

Freeport and Nassau both have extensive, modern deepwater ports.

Air

Because of the number of islands within The Bahamas, air travel is common and there are some 50 airports and airstrips, more than half of which are privately owned. As you land at either Freeport or Nassau you can see just how many private planes are used around the islands. There are also more than 20 seaplane ramps throughout The Bahamas. Bahamasair, the national airline, flies to all the main Out Islands, and while it may sound extravagant, it may work out cheaper for groups of four or more, to charter their own small plane for trips. Almost all flights are routed via Nassau, so if you want to travel around the islands, you will usually have to return to Nassau to take an onward flight.

Nassau itself is a lovely old colonial city that owes its prosperity to its natural harbor. It was settled in 1666, and originally called Charles Towne after the English King Charles II, but it changed its name when William III of Orange, and also of Nassau, came to the throne. In the past it has seen pirates and gunrunners, and more recently rumrunners breaking the US Prohibition. Today, it is a major port and cruise ship terminal, attracting more than a million cruise passengers a year.

The colonnaded warehouses lining the quay now house boutiques and restaurants, and the city has magnificent historic homes and public buildings, with tree-lined streets and horse drawn carriages which now convey tourists rather than freight as of old. One of the great attractions of Nassau is how the old and new merge with historic well-preserved buildings dwarfed by modern tower blocks and Government offices, leading world financial institutions and centuries old open-air markets. There are wonderful old colonial mansions, art deco homes perched on the hills, and the spectacular high rise luxury hotels on Cable Beach. It is busy year-round with tourists and business visitors and increasingly bankers and financiers.

The immaculately dressed police officers in their dazzling white jackets and topis (pith helmets) control the traffic in the main thoroughfares.

EXPLORING NASSAU

If you want to explore the city start at **Rawson Square** where there is a tourist information area. It is conveniently close to the **Prince George Dock and Wharf** where the cruise shops dock and disgorge their passengers, and it connects with historic **Bay Street** that runs inland parallel with the harbor. Also running level with Bay Street from Rawson Square is the short **Woodes Rogers Walk** that gives a taste of Nassau's seafaring past, and takes you to the **Nassau International Bazaar** on the corner with Charlotte Street.

The **Junkanoo Expo** on Nassau's water front, is the first museum of its kind to showcase the history of the parade and to give visitors a taste of it with displays of the highly original, ornate and vivid costumes, and sound tracks recorded during the event.

Bustling Bay Street is still the commercial heart of the city, and a must. The old buildings house some of the most elegant shops in The Bahamas offering a wide range of duty free goods, from perfume, china and crystal to cameras, jewels and leather goods, and much more. **The Straw Market** standing on the site of the original Charles Towne Market, was completely destroyed by fire in September 2001. It is being rebuilt and is a great place to buy woven straw goods, carvings, handicrafts and T-shirts.

Have your hair braided in the hair-braiding shop on Prince George Dock near the Cruise Ship Port. The market is in Market Plaza on Bay Street. In Rawson Square you can see the statue of Sir Milo Butler, the first Governor-General of The Bahamas. There are lots of interesting streets off Bay Street with shops and lively eateries, including Woodes Rogers Walk that runs down to the quayside.

Colonial hotel

At Number 1 Bay Street stands the grand **British Colonial Hilton Hotel**, once one of the flagship hotels of the British Empire and comparable with Raffles in Singapore. The six-floor pink and white building was opened in 1899 on the site of Fort Nassau, built in 1696, but burned down in 1921. It was rebuilt and opened in 1923 as the New Colonial Hotel and has changed hands many times, although it is still affectionately referred to by all as "the BC".

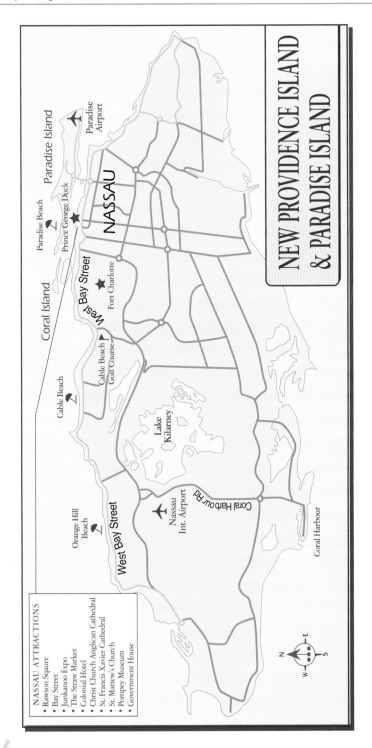

NEW PROVIDENCE ISLAND & PARADISE ISLAND

Paradise Island

Paradise Airport

Paradise Beach

Prince George Dock

NASSAU

Coral Island

West Bay Street

Fort Charlotte

Cable Beach

Cable Beach
Golf Course

Orange Hill Beach

Lake Kilarney

West Bay Street

Nassau Int. Airport

Coral Harbour Rd

Coral Harbour

NASSAU ATTRACTIONS
- Rawson Sqaure
- Bay Street
- Junkanoo Expo
- The Straw Market
- Colonial Hotel
- Christ Church Anglican Cathedral
- St. Francis Xavier Cathedral
- St. Mattew's Church
- Pompey Museum
- Government House

N
E
S
W

The busiest time of the year in Nassau and Paradise Island is during Junkanoo, The Bahamas version of Carnival, which is held on Boxing Day (26 December) and New Year's Day (1 January). It begins with pre-dawn costume parades from various parts of the city descending on downtown Nassau – the culmination of a year's hard work. Clubs, companies and groups work all year to come up with the most original, most vivid costumes, which are literally sculpted from crêpe paper and papier mâché. The parades are led by scores of drummers beating their goatskin drums, cowbell shakers, whistle blowers and rhythmic dancers, and the pulsating beat vibrates through the city and is impossible to ignore.

If you can't make it to Nassau for Junkanoo, you can get a taste of what the festival is like by visiting the Junkanoo Museum in Nassau, where there are displays of the bright costumes and tapes recorded from actual parades.

Other special events include: Goombay, Guy Fawkes Day, Independence Celebrations, Fox Hill Day, Regattas and Community Fairs, Seafood Festivals and Music Festivals.

Junkanoo Parade

The US Embassy is just round the corner in Queen Street, and opposite in George Street is the gothic **Christ Church Anglican Cathedral** built in 1837 on the site of a parish church. ☎ 322-3015.

Other interesting churches are **St. Francis Xavier Cathedral** on West Hill Street, completed in 1886 and the island's oldest Catholic Church, and **St. Matthew's Anglican Church**, on Church and Shirley Streets, built between1802 and 1804. There are two cemeteries, one next to the church, and the old cemetery just across the road and closer to the water with some very old stone tombs. Two of the country's national heroes – Sir Milo B. Butler, the first Bahamian Governor General and Sir Cecil Wallace-Whitfield, former leader of the governing Free National Movement, are buried in the church's cemetery.

Further down Bay Street and facing Rawson Square is Parliament Square. The statue of the young Queen Victoria sitting on her throne, and flanked by cannon, is in front of the pastel-shaded colonnaded buildings around Parliament Square that are the administrative heart of the city. Around the square are the **Senate, Chambers of Parliament and House of Assembly** where the Parliament meets. The public buildings, including the Supreme Court, are based on the design of Governor Tryon's Official Residence in New Bern, the former capital of North Carolina.

The **Supreme Court** offers a major tourist attraction four times a year – in January, April, July and October – when you can witness the traditional pomp and pageantry of the official opening of the Supreme Court Sessions. The judges in the wigs and gowns march in stately procession.

The octagonal **Nassau Public Library** in Shirley Street was built in 1800 and was the town prison until the late 1870s. The alcoves that now house books, were the old prison cells. The Archives are in Mackey Street and have a microfilm collection of historical documents dating back to 1700 as well as old pictures and maps.

The **Pompey Museum** is itself a piece of Bahamian history as it is on the site of the eighteenth-century slave market. It has a permanent display by the internationally acclaimed Bahamanian artist Amos Fergus, with 25 of his paintings on show in the first floor gallery. Another on-going exhibition is Road to Freedom: Slavery, Abolition and Emancipation, on the ground floor.

Balcony House, Market Street, is a beautifully restored eighteenth-century wooden mansion with period furnishings. It is believed to be the oldest wooden house in Nassau.

The **Bahamas National Historical Society Museum**, on Shirley Street and Elizabeth Avenue, gives a fascinating insight into the history of the islands with historical and cultural artifacts tracing the people from the pre-Columbian Arawak Indians to modern times. Almost a mile (1.6km) further east on Shirley Street is the Anglican St. Matthew's Church, built between 1800 and 1802 and consecrated in 1804. It is the oldest church in The Bahamas.

The pink **Government House**, Blue Hill Road, is also on top of the cliff with fabulous views, and only five minutes from downtown Nassau. It is the official residence of the Governor General, the personal representative of Queen

Commemorative steps

Climb the 65 steps up the **Queen's Staircase** to **Fort Fincastle** on top of the cliff. The steps were given their present name at the beginning of the twentieth century as each step was said to commemorate one year of Queen Victoria's reign. The steps were cut in the limestone cliff by slaves in the 1790s to provide direct access to the fort from the town, although some have suggested it was an escape route for the troops if the fort was about to fall. Fort Fincastle was built in 1793 by Governor Lord Dunmore in the shape of a ship, and is dominated by the 126ft (38m) tall water tower and lighthouse, which at 200ft (61m) above sea level, is the highest structure on the island. You can take the lift to the top of the tower for 50c and the views spanning the island are superb. You can look out over Nassau and Paradise Island, look down on Fort Fincastle below, and see across to the south coast. The fort still has many of its original canons – never fired in anger. There are guided tours of the fort daily.

Elizabeth II, the titular head of State, and was built in neoclassical style in 1801 with elegant columns, and typical louvered windows. It is the scene of the spectacular Changing of the Guard Ceremony that takes place on alternate Saturdays throughout the year. It is an event full of pomp and ceremony with music provided by the world famous Royal Bahamas Police Force Band. A statue of Columbus stands by the imposing steps that lead down from Government House to the street.

Opposite Government House is the Georgian-style **Graycliff,** formerly a private mansion, and now one of the island's top hotels with a splendid restaurant. It is said to have been built by a privateer called Gray whose ship was called Graywolf, and until the 1970s it was the private winter home of the Earl and Countess of Dudley.

Along the cliffs there are many other fine stone buildings, built in the nineteenth century by wealthy merchants on top of the hill so that they were separated from the masses below. On the hill above Government House is Gregory Arch, which marks the boundary between downtown 'wealthy' Nassau, and the poorer district over the hill in Grant's Town. Also worth visiting is the **Pirates Museum**, Marlborough and George Streets, with its multimedia and interactive displays including a replica pirate ship

From downtown Nassau you simply have to cross the toll Bridge to Paradise Island, but just before the bridge you must visit the busy fish, fruit and vegetable Market by Potter's Cay docks, where all manner of produce is sold from fruit and vegetables to conch and freshly landed fish. The weekly mail boats also sail from here.

Atlantis Showroom $$-$$$
Atlantis Paradise Island Casino
☎ 363-2518. Continental dining.
Reservations only.

Bahamian Club $$$
Paradise Island ☎ 363-2518. Fine
dining, impeccable meat.

Bahamian Kitchen $$
Trinity Place, Bay Street
☎ 325-0702. Island dishes.

Black Angus Grill $$-$$$
Nassau Marriott Resort
☎ 327-6200 Cable Beach, steak and
seafood.

Blue Marlin $-$$
Hurricane Hole Marina, Paradise
Island ☎ 363-2660. Bahamian.

Buena Vista $$$
Delancy Street ☎322-2811. Fine
French with excellent fish.

Café Casino $$
Atlantis Paradise Island Casino
☎ 363-2518. American-Bahamian.

Café Johnny Canoe $-$$
Nassau Beach ☎ 327-3373. Bahamian.

Café Martinique $$$
Paradise Island
☎ 363-2518. Luxury dining.

Captain Nemo's $$
Deveaux Street
☎ 323-8394. Seafood and steaks.

Caribe Café $$-$$$
British Colonial
☎ 322-3301. Seafood and Bahamian.

Chinese Kitchen $$
Nassau Street
☎ 322-2976. Chinese.

Colombo Yogurt $
Prince George Street, Bay Street
☎ 322-6311. Ice cream, snacks and
yogurt.

Coyaba $$
Paradise Island
☎ 363-3000. Good Chinese and
Polynesian.

Dockside Bar and Grill Café $$
Prince George Arcade
Bahamian, Greek and Italian.

Double Dragon $$
Mackey Street
☎ 393-5718. Chinese.

Flying Cloud $-$$
Paradise Island West Dock
☎ 393-1957. Bahamian.

Goombay Mama's $
Nassau Marriott Resort, Cable Beach .
☎ 327-6200.

Graycliff $$-$$$
West Hill Street
☎ 322-2796. Considered by many as
the finest dining in Nassau based on
classic French cuisine with a stunning
wine list.

Green Shutters $$
Parliament Street
☎ 325-5702. English-style pub in 200
year old building, Bahamian and
English dishes.

Gulfstream $$
Paradise Island
☎ 363-3000. Seafood.

Passin' Jacks $$
East Bay Street
☎ 393-0771. Steaks and seafood.

Junkanoo Café $
Bay Street and Colony Place
☎ 328-7944. American.

Japanese Steak House $$-$$$
Cable Beach
☎ 327-7781. Japanese.

Main Dining Room $$-$$$
Breezes
☎ 327-6153. International buffet.

Mama Liddy's Place $$
Market Street
☎ 322-4201. Island dishes.

Montagu Gardens Steak and Grill $$
East Bay Street,
☎ 394-6347.

Ocean Club $$$
Paradise Island
☎ 348-3615
Excellent continental and American.

Pick-a-Dilly $-$$
Parliament Square
☎ 322-2836
Seafood, pasta and Bahamian.

Poop Deck $$
East Bay Street
☎ 393-8175. Seafood and Bahamian
dishes, very lively and popular.

Shoal Restaurant and Lounge $-$$
Nassau Street
☎ 323-4400.
Bahamian and American cuisine.

Skans $$-$$
Bay Street
☎ 325-5536
Home made Bahamian and American.

Spices $$
Paradise Island
☎ 363-3000. Casual Bahamian.

Stars Restaurant and Deli $-$$
Circle Palm Malls
☎ 394-1692.

Sun And $$
Lakeview Avenue
☎ 393-1205
Elegant Continental and an impressive
clientele who appreciate the best.

Tony Roma's $$-$$$
Saunder's Beach and opposite Paradise
Island Bridge
☎ 325-2020. American.

Traveller's Rest $-$$
West Bay Street
☎ 327-7633
Bahamian dining by the sea.

Nightlife

Casinos
**Crystal Palace Casino and Atlantis
Resort and Casino.**

Discos
Club Pastishe, Beach Tower,
Paradise Island, ☎ 363-3000

Polka Dot Lounge, Radisson Grand
☎ 363-2011.

Shows
Junkanoo Jamboree,
Radisson Cable Beach ☎ 327-6000

Jubilation,
Crystal Palace ☎ 327-6200

King and Knights 11,
Nassau Beach Hotel ☎ 327-5321

Magical Voyage,
Rainforest Theatre, ☎ 327-6200

Blue Marlin,
Paradise Island ☎ 363-2660

Sunsation,
Atlantis Paradise Island,☎ 363-3000

Ronnie Butler Show,
Radisson Cable Beach ☎ 327-6000.

Others
Jokers Wild Comedy Club,
Paradise Island Casino ☎ 363-2000

Silk Cotton Jazz Club,
Market Street ☎ 356-0955

Club Waterloo,
Lake Waterloo ☎ 393-7324

200 Nightclub
West Bay Street ☎ 322-7195

2000 Nightclub,
Rock and Roll Café ☎ 327-7639

Dicky Mo's ☎ 327-7854

Rumour's ☎ 323-2925

Shooters ☎ 393-7324

The Zoo ☎ 322-7195

PARADISE ISLAND

Paradise Island was called Hog Island and was the home of many very wealthy people, including Joseph Lynch, co-founder of Merrill Lynch, and Dr Axel Wenner-Gren, the Swedish tycoon, who bought the island. His home is now the Café Martinique. In 1961 the island was purchased by Huntington Hartford, who changed the name to Paradise Island, imported the Cloisters, and set about developing the island as a luxury resort. Although ownership of the island has changed several times since, Paradise Island continues to be a major tourist destination.

Coral Island

You can visit the fourteenth-century French Augustinian Cloisters in **Versailles Gardens**, a popular wedding venue for both islanders and visitors. Although it is the oldest building in The Bahamas, it is something of an imposter, as all the stone was shipped in from Lourdes, France in the 1920s and the structure was rebuilt although there were no plans of the original to work from. It was then taken again and rebuilt on its present site in 1968. It is reached down a flight of steps between rows of statues in the Versailles Gardens, so called because of its formal lay out, fountains and statues, copied from its French namesake. The statue of Hercules in the pond in the middle of the gardens is believed to date from the twelfth century.

Nearby is the exclusive **Ocean Club** offering golf, tennis and delightful dockside gardens. Paradise Island is also the home of **Sun International's Atlantis Resort and Casino**, which offers even more choice of where to dine and be entertained, and there is the **Hurricane Hole Plaza** just inland from the marina, if you want to shop. The **Dig at**

Atlantis is a recreation of the legendary lost, underwater city. It is housed in the largest outdoor aquarium in the world. You can walk under the aquarium through glass tunnels.

AN ISLAND TOUR

If you head west out of Nassau city, you reach the moated **Fort Charlotte**, which was built by Lord Dunmore in the late 1780s to guard the western entrance to the harbor. It was named after the consort of George III, and cost so much that it became known as Dunmore's Folly. It had a drawbridge and massive ramparts, and boasted a formidable arsenal of more than 40 canons, but never fired its guns in anger. There are fine views over the port from its hilltop vantage point, and you can look out over man-made Arawak Cay, with its huge tanks that hold the city's drinking water brought in by barge from the Andros Islands. Below the fort is **Clifford Park** where many of the island's official ceremonies and major sporting events take place.

Then head for the waterfront and **Coral World** that is on Coral Island. You get there by crossing Arawak Cay with its traditional Bahamian food stalls and fish fries that are very popular with islanders and visitors alike during the evenings and weekends. Access to the island is over a single lane bridge, but you have to park by the bridge and take the courtesy bus that shuttles visitors between their vehicles and the attraction.

Coral World is an educational and entertainment theme park, covering 16 acres (6.5 hectares), with 24 aquaria, including shark, stingray and turtle tanks, as well as the 360° Encounter A Reef tank. It is set in landscaped parkland, and one of the star attractions is the underwater observation tower that allows visitors to see marine life 20ft (6m) below the surface in a natural sea environment. You can also climb the tower for views along the coast. The Wishing Well is believed to have been the island's only source of fresh water for the early Indians and marauding pirates. You can follow the Pleasure Reef snorkeling trail or spend time sunning yourself on the small white sand beach alongside the attraction. The property also has 22 secluded villas for rent, each with its own pool, and it offers a special honeymoon package.

Gardens to visit

Close by are the **Botanic Gardens** that cover 18 acres (7 hectares) off West Bay Street, and contain tropical trees, shrubs and flowering plants, as well as a replica of a Lucayan village. Also close by are the **Ardastra Gardens,** covering 5 acres (2 hectares) of landscaped gardens, and featuring more than 300 species of exotic birds, mammals and reptiles, including trained pink flamingoes, which march to order at their trainer's commands.

Continued on page 56...

Above: Coral Island Beach

Left: Coral Island, New Providence

Below: Coral Island, New Providence

Opposite page: Snorkeling on Coral Island

Most popular resort area

You then pass the usually busy **Saunders Beach** and **Brown's Point Beach** before arriving at **Cable Beach**, the island's main resort area. This luxury resort to the west of Nassau has mushroomed since the first hotels were built in the 1950s. It gets its name because the communications cable linking the island to Florida came ashore here. It has a fabulous beach, a wide range of accommodation to suit most budgets, and all manner of sports from golf and tennis to diving and water skiing. There are shops if you want to spend your money during the day, and casinos, if you want to try and win it back in the evening. Most of the hotels and casinos offer cabarets and other live entertainment, and there are also romantic moon-light dinner cruises and discos, or you can just enjoy a walk along the beach under the stars. It's most famous resort is **Nassau Marriott Resort** and **Crystal Palace Casino** with the **Cable Beach-Crystal Palace golf course** and action-packed vast casino. Next to the casino is a shopping arcade that connects it with the newly renovated **Radisson Cable Beach Resort**.

To the west of Cable Beach there is another popular straw market, then at Rock Point, you may be able to identify the pink house on the promontory, as another location for the James Bond Thunderball film. It was here in the two connected pools, that one of the villains was fed to the sharks for displeasing his boss.

Along West Bay Street you pass **The Lucayan Caves**, huge limestone caverns that have been etched out by the action of the tides. Indians are said to have lived in the caves and while they may have, there is no evidence to support this.

Conference Corner, just beyond the caves, gets its name because it was here in 1962 that President John F Kennedy, Prime Minister John Diefenbaker of Canada, and Prime Minister Harold Macmillan of Britain, each planted a tree to commemorate their summit meeting in Nassau. Inland from the caves is the huge **Lake Killarney**, and the smaller **Lake Cunningham**. There is canoeing on **Lake Nancy** (☎ 323-3382) and a canal leads into Lake Killarney.

The road then runs past **Love Beach** near the north-west corner of the island where there are many expensive private homes, including one formerly owned by interna-tional singing star Julio Iglesias. The coral area offshore is known as the **Sea Gardens** and you can take a glass-bottomed boat to marvel at its beauty.

After the international airport, you reach **Lyford Cay** on the west-ern tip of New Providence, and now one of the most exclusive and wealthy private residential develop-ments on the island with magnificent views. Sidney Poitier and Sean Connery have homes here. Lyford Cay Gallery, Lyford Cay Shopping Centre, is a museum and gallery fea-turing art from around the world.

The western half of the island is far quieter than the east and the wildlife teems in the woodlands and coastal areas. There are lots of deserted beaches to explore. **Clifton Pier** used to be where the cruise ships docked, but the area is now more popular as home of Kalik beer, which is made at the **Commonwealth Brewery** (☎ 362-4789).

The south coast is more traditional with a number of small settlements, such as **Adelaide Village** that was settled originally by freed Africans, as were Gambier and Fox Hill.

Home of Bacardi

The coast road then runs past Corry Sound and Millar's Sound to one of the most popular attractions on the south coast, the **Bacardi Rum Distillery** that can be toured and its products sampled. Until about 130 years ago rum was unrefined and a harsh spirit until a wine merchant in Santiago de Cuba produced the world's first light rum in 1862, and gave it his family's name – Bacardi. Don Facundo Bacardi used special yeast in the fermentation and then further mellowed his spirit by ageing in oak casks. Finally, the rum received a second charcoal filtering to impart its unique smoothness and dryness. Today, the distillery produces a range of rums from white to light, and dark to flavored. **Guests arriving at Nassau International Airport during peak times are usually greeted with a free glass of Bacardi to welcome them to the island.**

The road then cuts inland past Bonefish Pond and Cay Point to the southeastern corner of the island and **Fox Hill**. The residents of Fox Hill did not hear about the declaration of Emancipation until seven days after the news had been known in Nassau, and they still celebrate the event one week after everyone else. Their festivities take place on the second Tuesday of August and it is a fun time with lots of music, art and home cooking – it is a good idea because it allows everyone to celebrate twice.

Further inland is **St Augustine's Monastery**, the home of a community of Benedictine monks and built by Father Jerome. He also built the Hermitage on Mt. Alvernia, Cat Island where he is buried. The monastery is set in lovely tropical gardens that you can visit.

Return to the coast road that then runs east, past Eastern Point and Blackbeard's Tower on the hill. Despite the legends, it is probably just an old stone water tower, although it does offer great views and would have made a good look out point.

On the eastern coast is **The Retreat**, the headquarters of the Bahamas National Trust. The 5 acres (2 hectares) of manicured grounds contain more than 200 species of palms, other trees and plants.

You return to Nassau past the Nassau **Yacht Haven** and **Fort Montagu**, built in 1741 from local limestone. The only action it saw was during the American Revolutionary War when it was overrun by rebel troops led by John Paul Jones. They held the fort for two weeks before slipping away. The fort is open and you can just wander around. The nearby **Montagu Bay** has fine beaches and hosts many yachting regattas.

GRAND BAHAMA

Grand Bahama is 55 miles (89km) east of Florida's Palm Beach, 80 miles (129km) long and 16 miles (26 km) across at its widest point, making it the fourth largest island in The Bahamas. It covers 530 sq miles (1379 sq km), and has a population of 50,000, and includes the city of Freeport/Lucaya, and the resort area of West End. Its nearest islands are the Abaco Islands to the east, and the Bimini Islands to the south.

Gold Rock Beach, Grand Bahama

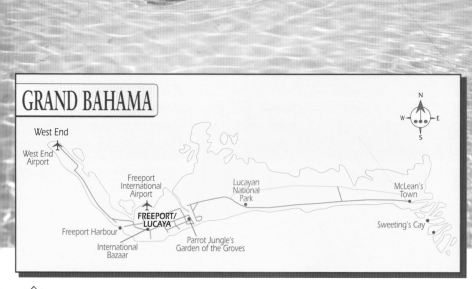

GRAND BAHAMA

West End

West End Airport

Freeport International Airport

Lucayan National Park

McLean's Town

FREEPORT/ LUCAYA

Sweeting's Cay

Freeport Harbour

International Bazaar

Parrot Jungle's Garden of the Groves

N W E S

History of Grand Bahama

Until the 1950s, the island was not much more than a collection of quiet, picturesque fishing villages with a long, exciting and sometimes, shady history – pirates and in the 1920s, a haven for rumrunners breaking the US Prohibition. In the 1950s, however, a group of industrialists led by American Wallace Groves and Briton Sir Charles Hayward acquired 200 sq miles (520 sq km) near the heart of the island, and set about creating the Caribbean's first planned city – Freeport. It had a modern and very busy port and cruise ship dock, tax free status, new industries, an airport and most important, tourism development. Ever since, Grand Bahama, just a 30-minute flight from Florida, has been The Bahamas' most popular destination because it offers so much, from the glitz and glamour of Freeport shopping and nightlife, to delightfully landscaped Lucaya, stunning beaches and the spectacular beauty of the unspoiled Lucayan National Park and the eastern half of the island.

The island is mostly composed of limestone that is porous and water erosion has led to the creation of scores of underground caves. The subterranean rock also stores considerable reserves of fresh water, despite a relatively low annual rainfall – about 57in (145cm) a year.

On Grand Bahama, there is never any excuse for getting bored – at any time of the day or the night. You can laze on the beach all day or go sightseeing, you can spend a few hours trying out your luck in the casinos, or you can take part in a huge variety of sports, both water

Left: Port Lucaya Market Place

Below: Bahamas Princess Casino and Resort, Freeport

and land based. There are golf courses, more than 50 tennis courts, many of them floodlit; you can ride horseback along the beach or explore inland by bike. The beaches are spectacular and the warm, turquoise waters and offshore reefs offer world-class scuba diving and snorkeling.

Although Freeport and the resort areas are as cosmopolitan as you are likely to find anywhere, there are still large areas of the island where you can get away from the crowds, enjoy your own stretch of white sand beach or explore magnificent wilderness areas and delightful countryside villages. The southern coast contains many secluded beaches, inlets and picturesque little fishing villages. Many people consider East End with its secluded creeks and deserted bays, mangroves and rich wildlife, the most beautiful part of the island, although the journey from McLean's Town, the most easterly settlement accessible by road, has to be continued by boat.

There really is a host of things to do at any time of the day or night, at any time of the year, but things get really lively at the end of August when the Goombay Summer Festival is celebrated, and over Christmas, when the Junkanoo Festival takes place on December 26 and January 1. Both festivals run over several days and are packed with costume parades and street parties, special events and sporting activities, and lots and lots of dancing, wining and dining.

TRANSPORT ON THE ISLAND

Buses operate in Freeport/Lucaya and to nearby villages. Taxis are plentiful, and most hotels operate their own shuttle service, especially to the airport.

FREEPORT

Freeport/Lucaya is the second largest city in The Bahamas and a bustling tourist resort with a wide range of accommodation from international-class hotels to small, intimate inns and self-catering apartments. Although the Freeport-Lucaya conurbation is always linked and looks like one city on the map, the two communities are in fact, about seven miles apart, and too far to walk in the heat, so you need to take a taxi or bus to travel between them.

The wide, palm tree-lined boulevards have big name boutiques, duty free shops and galleries. The **International Bazaar**, in East Mall Drive in the heart of Freeport, boasts more than 90 shops, top name boutiques such as Gucci and Fendi, and restaurants, with goods and cuisine from 25 countries. You cannot miss the entrance that is dominated by the huge 35ft (8m) tall red-lacquer Japanese Shinto temple gate, known as a *torii*, a traditional sign of welcome in Japan. Bargains range from the finest crystal, lace and jewels to cameras, perfume and local crafts, including excellent hand-batik clothing. Next to the International Bazaar is the bright and bustling **Straw Market**, which is one of the best places to buy local arts and crafts, and an opportunity to bargain over prices, which is all part of the process so do not be embarrassed to haggle. Here you will find woven goods, and items made from wood, shells and other natural island materials.

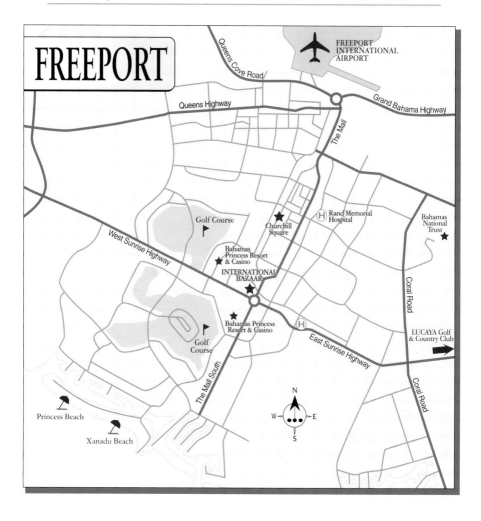

A short distance away is **Churchill Square,** the commercial heart of the city, and nearby is the **Rand Memorial Hospital.** The **Court House** is just round the corner in Pioneers Way. If you are self catering, you can use the grocery shops around Churchill Square with other shopping opportunities at the malls at the **Regent Centre.**

The **Port Lucaya Marketplace** is one of the island's newest shopping malls, covering 6 acres (2.3 hectares), with about 80 shops, restaurants, traditional English pubs and entertainment. The shops are grouped together in clusters in an attractive park setting centered on **Count Basie Square,** and beside the **Bell Channel Marina.** The park is often the venue for free concerts and there is a bandstand in the square. There is a choice of restaurants, fast food outlets and an English-style pub called Fatman's Nephew that is very lively in the evening. You can also visit the unusual **Ye Olde Bottle Museum** that has hundreds of antique bottles dating back to 1650. There is another busy, Straw market just outside the marketplace, with the beautiful Lucaya beaches nearby.

THINGS TO SEE AND DO

Parrot Jungle's Garden of the Groves covers 12 acres (4.8 hectares) and contains thousands of rare trees and exotic plants and shrubs, most of them tagged for identification. It was a bequest of American Wallace Grove, one of the original developers, and there is a delightful lake with waterfalls, ponds, streams and a grotto, which has become a very popular spot for island weddings. The Garden is also the home of a petting zoo and the **Grand Bahama Museum** where you can explore the island's history from pre-Columbian times to the present. Of special interest are some Lucayan skulls found in caves on the island. The skulls have very flat tops, and one suggestion is that the Indians deliberately flattened the tops of their babies heads by strapping boards to them, to toughen the skulls to make them better able to withstand club attacks by the Caribs.

INDOOR AND OUTDOOR SPORT

GAMBLING

The island has two casinos, at the **Bahamas Princess Resort and Casino**, and the **Lucayan Beach Resort and Casino**. Apart from the chance to try your luck, both casinos offer fine dining and spectacular cabaret shows.

GOLF

Grand Bahama boasts three of the finest championship golf courses in the Caribbean. The Ruby and Emerald Courses are at the **Bahamas Princess Resort and Casino**, and the third is at the **Lucayan Golf and Country Club**, and there is a 9-hole course at the **Fortune Hills Golf and Country Club**.

The 6,824-yard par-72 Lucaya course is the island's oldest, built in 1963 and designed by Dick Wilson. The 6,679-yard par-72 Emerald course was also built by Dick Wilson and opened in 1965. The 6,750-yard par-72 Ruby course winds its way through lush forest, and was designed and built by Joe Lee in 1967.

Hawksbill Creek, to the west of Freeport/Lucaya is the island's industrial heart, close to **Freeport Harbour** where ships, tankers and cruise liners dock. There is a busy fish market. The **Hydroflora Gardens** are fascinating because lush vegetation and tropical plants are all grown in a soil-free environment.

Lucayan National Park Beach, 40 acre (16 hectare) to the east of Freeport with its underwater caves, forest trails and secluded beach, includes the longest known underwater cave and cavern system in the world, with over 6 miles (10km) of caves and tunnels so far charted. Many of the sheltered rock pools contain rare marine species. A spiral staircase leads down into the underground cavern system and **Ben's Cave**, named after Freeport diver Ben Rose who explored it. Close by is **Burial Cave** where the bones of pre-Columbian Indians were found on the cave floor under water. Above ground, every type of vegetation zone seen in The Bahamas can be found, and there is a boardwalk path through pine forest and mangrove creek to **Gold Rock Beach**, one of the most beautiful on the island.

McLean's Town is on the eastern coast and is home of the annual Conch Cracking Contest, held on 12 October – Discovery Day. The contestants race to open as many conch shells as possible and extract their contents. It is the most easterly settlement that can be reached by road, and to travel on to **Sweetings Cay, Lightbourne Cay and East End Point** you have to travel by boat.

Visit the **Perfume Factory** set in a replica of an eighteenth-century Georgian Bahamas mansion, and create your own fragrance. You can see perfumes being created, learn about Bahamian spices and flowers used for their scents sample island-made fragrances, create your own exclusive perfume, and have it bottled and personally labeled (☎ 352-9391).

Peterson Cay National Park is a 1.5-acre (.6 hectare) park that includes the only cave on Grand Bahama's leeward shore. It is an area of outstanding natural beauty, and very popular with the islanders over the weekend. The cay is one mile (1.6km) off Barbary Beach off the Old Freetown Road.

Smith's Point is one of the many small fishing communities on the island which have changed little over the past 100 years, and which is still inhabited by Smiths. Along the coast you will find **Pinder's Point, Williams Town, Russell Town** and **Martin Town**, all named after their founding family, and still all boasting their descendants. Smith's

Unusual wood

The **Rand Nature Centre**, off East Settler's Way, is run by the Bahamas National Trust and covers 100 acres (40 hectares) of woodland with well-marked trails, native plants and a collection of wild orchids, many of them tiny plants. The reserve also has a large bird population, including humming birds and West Indian flamingos. A traditional log and thatch Lucayan village is close to a stand of Bahamian braziletto wood, one of the hardest and most expensive of timbers. It is said that in the 1600s, settlers on Eleuthera were given aid by the New England colony, and in gratitude they sent them a consignment of 10 tons of braziletto. The wood was sold and the money raised was used to help found Yale University.

Point is famous for Mama Flo's restaurant that specializes in island home cooking, with dishes like cracked conch, steam fish and peas'n rice, washed down with the excellent local Kailik beer.

Theo's Wreck is a popular dive site off Freeport. The 230ft (70m) freighter was sunk in 1982 in 100ft (30m) of water to provide a dive site on the edge of the Grand Bahama Ledge with a 2,000ft (610.m) drop off.

The **TodHunter Mitchell Distillery** on Queen's Highway, produces 100,000 cases of rum a year. Apart from traditional rums, it also produces flavored rums, with mango one of the latest flavors. It has been owned by Bahamian wine merchants Butler and Sands since 1944. It is not open to the public although its products are widely available (☎ 352-6627).

The **Underwater Explorers' Society (UNEXSO),** next to Port Lucaya, offers the chance to learn the basics of scuba diving right up to dive master and instructor level, and also the opportunity to swim with dolphins. It is a full PADI/NAUI certified dive shop, and the society, which has been operating for 30 years, is one of the premier dive facilities in the region, let alone The Bahamas. It offers a three-hour introductory scuba course and snorkeling tuition in training pools, with equipment provided, and later in the day you can dive with your instructor on to a shallow reef. There are daily dive tours to the reefs, The Wall and shipwrecks, including night dives, and you can help UNEXSO divers feed the big reef sharks at the appropriately named Shark Junction.

UNEXSO has been at the forefront of both adventure diving and marine conservation in The Baha-

Swim with dolphins

The **UNEXSO's Dolphin Experience ™** is a 20-minute boat ride away at Sanctuary Bay, and allows selected visitors the chance to swim with bottle-nosed dolphins and learn more about these friendly and intelligent mammals. This is not a dolphin show, but part of the largest dolphin observation, training and research facility in the world. You can get magnificent close-up pictures, talk to the trainers and dangle your feet in the water to let the dolphins touch them. You can also wade in a 30in (75cm) deep tank and interact with the dolphins in the water. For a price you can also spend 15-20 minutes swimming with the dolphins in the calm waters of Sanctuary Bay, snorkel with them in open water, or be an assistant trainer for one, two or more days (☎ 373-1250).

mas for many years. It has been responsible for many of the mooring buoys over popular dive sites so that visiting boats don't have to drop anchor and damage the fragile reef and marine environment. There is also a photo -video center, equipment shop and boutique, and the Brass helmet Restaurant on the first floor that looks out over the dock (☎ 1-888-365-3483 [from US and Canada] or 373-1244).

The **Heritage Trail** runs from Old Freetown to Eight Mile Rock and is a delightful 5-mile (8km) long nature walk.

West End is the island's most westerly settlement, 28 miles (45km) from Freeport. It is a fishing village and a growing tourist area with several good restaurants offering genuine Bahamaian cuisine.

THE WEST END MOVE

Every Saturday West End is one of the liveliest places in the islands when it hosts West End Move, a typical West Indian street party that starts mid-morning and lasts until the last person decides its time for bed – or breakfast. Although it has become a major tourist attraction, the festivities are in no way artificial and are similar to those taking place on scores of islands throughout the Caribbean at the end of the working week. It is a time for unwinding, for partying, dancing, feasting and fun. Admission to the street party is free, and transport is laid on from most of the island's hotels to get you there – and back.

Most of the action takes place along Bayshore Road that runs from the village to the cove. There are sculling races across the harbor, very animated domino tournaments (remember that Bahamian domino players are among the best in the world), checkers, pool and a host of other games. You can take a boat out and try and catch your supper, hunt for conch, have your hair braided, see arts and crafts being made and buy those that catch your eye, and, of course, there is the food. West End is noted for its restaurants, but on Saturday night, food stalls spring up along the road offering the freshest of seafood and village delicacies. You should try 'love water' which is a herbal tea with reputed 'romantic' properties, and Coconut Jimmies, a delicious dessert.

West End Move, however, is noted above all for the music. The village calypso bands and local folk groups perform, music blasts out from speakers mounted in doorways and in the street, and even the most inhibited visitors will find their feet tapping and that suddenly, they are up and dancing alongside the thousands of other party goers. The West End Move is one party you will not forget in a hurry.

Eating out is one of the many pleasures of Grand Bahama because the quality is excellent and the choice enormous. You can dine on the finest international gourmet dishes, or enjoy wonderfully fresh, spicy local fare.

Alfredo's $$-$$$
Clarion Atlantik
☎ 373-1444. Italian.

Arawak Dining Room $$-$$$
Lucayan Golf Club
☎ 373-1066
French with Bahamian flare.

Banana Bay $-$$
Fortune Beach
☎ 373-2960. Seafood and Bahamian.

Barracuda's $$
Lucaya Reef Village
☎ 373-1333
International and Caribbean cuisine.

Becky's $-$$
Entrance to International Bazaar
☎ 352-8717. Bahamian.

Le Bouquet $$$
Radisson Lucaya Beach
☎ 373-1333
Fine French-Bahamian dining, reservations recommended.

Big G's $$
Pinder's Point
☎ 353-7124. Seafood.

Brass Helmet $$
over UNEXSO
☎ 373-2032. Lucaya, Bahamian and American dishes.

Britannia Bar $$
King's Road, Lucaya
☎ 373-5919
Fun pub food, Bahamian and Greek.

Buccaneer Club $-$$
Holmes Rock
☎ 349-3794. Fun beachside dining, seafood, Bahamian.

China Palace $-$$
International Bazaar.
☎ 352-7661

Cowboy's Barbecue $$
Port Lucaya Marketplace
☎ 373-9100
French, continental, dinner only.

Crown Room $$$
Bahamas Princess Casino
☎ 352-7811
Excellent, intimate dining, American and Continental.

Flamingo Beach Club $$
Bahamia Beach
☎ 352-3649. Bahamian/American.

Garden Café $$
Casino at Bahamia
☎ 352-7811. Open all day and late.

Geneva's Place $$
East Mall Drive
☎ 352-5085
Bahamian and American.

Guanahani's $$
Bahamas Princess Resort
☎ 352-6721
Seafood, Bahamian and American.

Islander's Roost $-$$
Ranfurly Circus
☎ 352-5110
Bahamian, American and seafood.

Junkanoo Bar $-$$
Port Lucaya Market Place
☎ 373-6170. Bahamian and seafood.

La Trattoria $$
Tower at Bahamia
☎ 350-7000
Italian – dinner only.

Lobster Reef Restaurant $$-$$$
Port Lucaya
☎ 373-8600. Seafood and steaks.

Margaretville Sand Bar $$
Mather Town
☎ 373-4525
Lively local fare.

Outrigger's $-$$
Smith's Point
☎ 373-4811
Seafood and Bahamian.

Palmetto Café $$
Parrot Jungle's Garden of the
Groves
☎ 373-5668. Bahamian/American.

Pier One $$
Freeport Harbour
☎ 352-6674
International.

Pisces $-$$
Bishop Place, Lucaya
☎ 373-5192
Seafood and pizza.

Shenanigan's $$
Port Lucaya Marketplace
☎ 373-4734
Irish/continental cuisine.

Stoned Crab $$
Taino Beach
☎ 373-1442
Great seafood.

The Surfside Restaurant
$$-$$$
Taino Beach
☎ 373-1814
Great seafood, especially conch,
grouper, snapper and lobster. The
restaurant is right on the beach, and
if you have the time, you can work
off your meal, or build up an
appetite for it, on the volleyball
court alongside.

Zobra's $$
Port Lucaya Marketplace
☎ 373-6137
Greek.

Nightlife

There is lots of choice from live
entertainment, discos, bars and
nightclubs.

Casinos

Lucayan Beach Casino
☎ 373-7777

Bahamas Princess Casino
☎ 352-6721.

Live Entertainment – most hotels,
Port Lucaya Marketplace.

Bahamas Princess Casino & Resort

New Providence and Paradise Island

Junkanoo Expo

Open: daily from 10am to 4.30pm.
There is a small admission charge.
☎ 356-2731.

The Doongalik Studios Gallery

Village Road
The island's premier showcase for
Junkanoo Art and Culture.
☎ 394-1886.

The Supreme Court

The courts are in session Monday to
Friday between 10am and 4pm.
☎ 322-7500.

Nassau Public Library

Shirley Street
Open: Monday to Friday between
10am and 9pm, and on Saturday
from 10am to 5pm.
☎ 322-4907.

The Archives

Mackey Street
Open: from Monday to Friday
between 10am and 4.45pm.
☎ 393-2175.

Pompey Museum

Open: Monday to Wednesday between
10am and 4pm, and Friday and
Saturday from 10am to noon.
☎ 326-2566.

Balcony House

Market Street
Open: Monday, Wednesday and
Friday from 10am to 1pm and 2pm
to 4pm.
☎ 326-2566.

The Bahamas National Historical Society Museum

Shirley Street and Elizabeth Avenue
Open: Monday to Friday from 10am
to 4pm and on Saturday from 10am
to noon (closed Thursday). There is a
small admission charge.
☎ 322-4231.

Government House

Blue Hill Road
The event takes place at 10am on
alternate Saturdays.
☎ 322-1875.

Pirates Museum

Marlborough and George Streets
Open: from 9am to 5 pm Monday to
Saturday
☎ 356-3759.

Fort Charlotte

West of Nassau
There are tours of the fort every half
hour from 9am to 4.30pm.
☎ 325-9186.

Botanic Gardens

off West Bay Street
Open: daily from 9am to 4.30pm.
☎ 323-5975.

Ardastra Gardens

There are marching shows at 11am,
2pm and 4pm, and the Gardens are
open daily from 9am to 5pm.
☎ 323-5806.

Coral World

Open: daily from 9am to 6pm.
☎ 328-1036.

Lyford Cay Gallery

Lyford Cay Shopping Centre
Museum and gallery featuring art from
around the world.
Open: Monday to Friday from 9am to
5.30pm and on Saturday from 9am to
5pm.
☎ 362-4040.

Bacardi Rum Distillery

Open: from Monday to Thursday from
9am to 4pm and on Friday between
9.30am and 3pm.
☎ 362-1412

St Augustine's Monastery

You can buy their excellent home made
guava jelly.
☎ 364-1331.

The Retreat

On the eastern coast
There are tours from Tuesday to
Thursday.
☎ 323-1317.

Atlantis Submarine

Pleasant Bay.
There is a shuttle bus from Nassau and
the resort areas to the Submarine dock
on the west of the island.
☎ 362-5676.

Seaworld Explorer

A mini sub that takes you on a
breathtaking cruise of the reefs, Athol
Island
☎ 356-2548.

Hartley's Undersea Walk

A special diving helmet lets you walk
on the sea floor.
☎ 393-8234.

Bahamas Bungee Jumping

East Bay Street, Club Waterloo
☎ 393-7324.

Calypso Getaway Cruise

Sails from Paradise Island by the
bridge
☎ 363-3577.

Dolphin Encounter and Stingray City

Blue Lagoon Island.
Blue Lagoon Island has featured in lots
of films including Splash, and it is a
20-minute boat ride from Nassau, with
lovely beaches, nature trails and
thousands of palms. The Dolphin
Encounter offers a number of ways to
interact with these intelligent and
playful mammals. You can wade out to
meet them in waist deep water, swim
or scuba with them. Stingray City
allows you to swim with the gentle
giant rays in a 3-acre marine park that
teems with other fish life, or you can
just visit the island for the day, laze on
the beach and enjoy a tropical buffet
lunch.

The island is open daily from 8am to
5pm.
☎ 363-6711/363-3179.

Seaplane Safaris

Offers the chance to view New
Providence from the air or visit the
Out Islands.
☎ 393-2552 or 393-1179 up to 10pm.

GRAND BAHAMA

The Regency Theatre

Grand Bahama
An island tradition staging several
productions each year .
☎ 352-5533.

Ye Olde Bottle Museum

Grand Bahama
Has hundreds of antique bottles
dating back to 1650.
Open: daily from 10am to 6pm.
☎ 373-2000.

Parrot Jungle's Garden of the Groves

The Garden is also the home of a
petting zoo and the Grand Bahama
Museum.
The gardens and museum are open
daily from 9am to 4pm.
☎ 373-5668.

Hydroflora Gardens

Fascinating because the lush
vegetation and tropical plants are all
grown in a soil-free environment.
The gardens are open daily.
☎ 352-6052.

Lucayan National Park Beach

It is always open.
☎ 352-5438.

The Rand Nature Centre

A great place to relax and enjoy the
nature walks.
There are guided tours at 10am, 2pm
and 3pm Monday to Friday and 2pm,
and 3pm on Sunday.
☎ 352-5438.

Exploring the Out Islands – Family Islands

The Out Islands really refer to all the islands of The Bahamas other than Grand Bahama and New Providence Island and their immediate offshore islands. In all there are almost 700 islands and cays, most of them uninhabited, and many of them offering near idyllic unspoiled beauty and seclusion. There are miles of deserted sandy beaches washed by warm, turquoise seas calmed by spectacular offshore reefs. There is very diverse vegetation ranging from pine forests and mangrove swamps in the north to palm trees and cacti in the south, all with a wealth of wildlife. The islands offer one of the few spots on earth where you can watch the West Indian flamingo, the white crowned pigeon and endangered Bahama parrot. There are rare terns, giant land crabs, and even larger rock iguanas, growing up to 6ft (2km) in length. There is also an amazing range of tropical flowering plants such as poinciana, hibiscus, oleander and the Bahamian national flower, yellow elder.

You can swim, dive and fish, or charter your own plane or boat and fly or sail across to your own desert island. The Abaco Islands are known as the sailing capital of the world, while Bimini is considered by many to be the sport fishing capital of the world.

All sizes and types of boat are available for charter, and most hotels have their own or can easily arrange boat hire. Many of the larger hotels have their own docks for guests arriving in their own vessels. The Green Turtle Club and Marina in The Abaco has 35 slips, while Valentine's Yacht Club and Inn on Harbour Island has 39 slips and can accommodate vessels up to 165ft (50m) in length. Flying is another excellent way of getting around and offers stunning views into the bargain. There are 45 airports and landing strips in the Out islands, and 15 have official ports of entry with customs and immigration facilities. Many hotels also have their own airstrips for guests.

There are scores of caves to be explored, historic sites and old buildings to be visited, and on those islands with communities, there is a warm and genuine welcome. It is no wonder that the Out Islands are often called the Family Islands, because you are immediately made to feel at home. There are more than 57 resorts on the 11 inhabited Out Islands, and accommodation ranges from luxury resorts to small hotels, delightful quaint inns to romantic cottages.

VISITING THE OUT ISLANDS

By air

Bahamasair flies to all the main Out islands from Nassau, there are scheduled services from Miami to some of the Out Islands, and also from Orlando, Palm Beach and Fort Lauderdale to Abaco, Andros, Bimini, Eleuthera, Exuma, Great Harbour, Long Island, San Salvador and Walker's Cay.

There are less frequent flights to the smaller islands with airstrips, but they still fly regularly and planes, including seaplanes, are always available for private charter.

By boat

There is a huge range of boats available for charter either bare boat or crewed, and mail boats regularly ply between the islands starting from Nassau and Freeport.

THE ABACO ISLANDS

The Abaco Islands cover 650sq miles (1690sq km), stretch in a curve for almost 130 miles (210km), have a population of about 11,000, and are famous for boat building and yachting. They include Great Abaco, covering 372sq miles (970sq km), Little Abaco, Elbow Cay, Great Guana Cay, Walker's Cay, Treasure Cay, Green Turtle Cay, Gorda Cay, Spanish Cay, Man O'War Cay and Pelican Cays.

Walker's Cay is the most northerly island in The Bahamas and has long been noted for its world-class deep-sea fishing. Its most unusual attraction is the Spiral Cavern. It has a resident population of more than 20 sharks which more than doubles at feeding times. The area to the west of the islands is the **Sea of Abaco** and is very popular with cruising yachts because the waters are calm, the islands acting as a barrier against the Atlantic Ocean.

On Little Abaco there are the picturesque settlements of **Fox Town** and **Crown Haven**. You can often see dolphins and whales off shore.

The islands have lots of wide-open spaces and many of the smaller cays are uninhabited, so it is the ideal place if you really want to get off the beaten track. Large areas in the south have been declared the **Abaco National Park** to protect the habitat of the ground nesting Abaco Parrot. The parrot is spectacular in flight with its blue and yellow wings. You can also spot the rare reddish egret, pelicans, humming birds, spoonbills, blue herons and white crowned pigeon, and among the trees you might glimpse wild boar and wild horses in the area around **Bahamas Star Farms** which grow citrus.

Today, the gaily painted pastel, clapboard houses and white picket fences, especially around the north

Travel on the Abaco Islands

There are three airports – at Walker's Cay in the north, Treasure Cay in the middle of the chain, and Marsh Harbour, the largest, in the south, and Spanish Cay for private pilots. There are ports of entry for yachts at Green Turtle Cay, Marsh Cay, Sandy Point, Spanish Cay and Walker's Cay, and the mail boats from Nassau visit several communities on Abaco.

There are taxis for getting around on land, several car rentals as well as water taxis and ferry for inter-island travel and boat rentals. Treasure Cay Shuttle plies between Treasure Cay Hotel Resort and Marsh Harbour Ferry Dock and the Abaco Beach Resort. Abaco Adventurers provides ferry service to Guana Cay, Man-o-War Cay and Treasure Cay Marina.

History of the Abaco Islands

It is the second largest island group in The Bahamas, and was visited by Ponce de Leon in 1513 but little happened for the next 250 years. It has a certain New England charm about it, which is not surprising as many of the first settlers were loyalists from the American colonies – South Carolina and Cape Cod – in 1783. After the American Revolution many loyalists from New England accepted land grants from the English crown to settle in The Bahamas, and they chose the Abaco Islands.

side of Green Turtle Cay are reminiscent of many New England small coastal towns and Cape Cod fishing villages, although they have the extra charm of graceful palms, tropical trees and beautiful exotic flowers, against the back drop of a shimmering turquoise sea. Of special interest, are the coral gardens on the reefs off Green Turtle Cay, and the picture postcard fishing village of **New Plymouth** at the southern tip of the island. The salt-box houses are beautifully kept, and painted in assorted pastel shades, behind their white picket fences. The New Plymouth Inn displays the intricate fretwork that is typical of nineteenth-century island architecture, and you should visit Miss Emily's Blue Bee Bar, on Victoria Street, whose island cocktails, especially goombay smash are legendary (☎ 365-4181).

You should visit the lovely white clapboard **Albert Lowe Museum** on

Parliament Street, which traces the island's history. It is in a refurbished Victorian home and has exhibits of maps, model ships built by Albert Lowe, and paintings by his son Alton.

The **Loyalist Memorial Sculpture Garden** has busts of about 30 Bahamians who have played a major role in the development of the Islands. Many of these were shipbuilders or sailors, traditions proudly continued on The Abaco Islands today, although tourism is now the major industry. One of the year's most popular events, however, is The Bahama Cup Regatta, held at the **Green Turtle Yacht Club** each July. Another major sailing event is Regatta Time in Abaco held in Marsh Harbour each July. There are many pleasant walks on Green Turtle Cay past grazing goats and strutting roosters, and among bright displays of tropical flowers.

Marsh Harbour on Great Abaco, is the largest town in the Abaco islands, and the third largest in The Bahamas, with an industrial base of shipbuilding and timber. It has an international airport, modern shopping area, several hotels and a spectacular shoreline. It also boasts the only traffic light on the island, and a 165-slip marina that attracts yachts and boats from around the world. There are shops and souvenir stands selling local arts and crafts, and some really good restaurants offering local specialties such as turtle steaks, wild boar and the freshest conch fritters. Apart from the pretty clapboard houses and cottages, there are several hotels and villas on the beach. Dr Evans Cottman, author of *Out Island Doctor*, lived in the turreted house above the town.

Abaco Inn Restaurant $$
Elbow Cay
☎ 366-0133. Bahamian and American
cuisine, reservations preferred.

Ambassador Inn $$
Marsh Harbour
☎ 367-2022. Local.

Angler's Restaurant $-$$
Hope Town
☎ 366-0087
Bahamian and continental.

Boat House $$
Elbow Cay
☎ 366-0065. Open all day, snacks and
local dishes.

Bluff House Restaurant $$-$$$
Green Turtle Cay
☎ 365-4247. Excellent candlelit
dining, reservations required.

Cap'n Jacks $$
Hope Town
☎ 366-0247
Bahamian dishes available all day.

Captain's Table $$-$$$
New Plymouth Club
☎ 365-4161
Bahamian and International dishes,
reservations required.

Club Soleil $$-$$$
Hope Town
☎ 366-0003. Bahamian fare and
noted Sunday champagne brunch.

Dockside Pavilion $$
Marsh Harbour
☎ 367-2319. Local and seafood.

Ena's $
Man-o-War-Cay
☎ 365-6187. Snacks and ice cream.

Gina's Restaurant $-$$
Great Abaco
☎ 367-3981. Traditional Bahamian,
try the turtle steaks.

Golden Grouper $$
Dove Plaza, Marsh Harbour
☎ 367-2301
Seafood and Bahamian.

Green Turtle Club $$-$$$
Green Turtle Cay
☎ 365-4271. Gourmet dining,
member of the Chaine des
Rotisseurs, reservations required.

Guana Beach Restaurant $$-$$$
Great Guana Beach Resort
☎ 365-5133
Fine international dining.

Harbour Lights $$
Great Abaco Beach Resort
☎ 367-2871. Bahamian dishes.

Harbour's Edge $$
Elbow Cay
☎366-0087. Local.

Jib Room $$-$$$
Pelican Shores, Marsh Harbour
☎ 367-2700. Seafood lunches and
international dishes at dinner.

Laura's Kitchen $-$$
New Plymouth
☎ 365-4287. Seafood and Bahamian.

Lobster Trap $-$$
Walker's Cay
☎ 352-5252
Seafood, snacks and fast food.

Lovely's Pizza $
Marsh Harbour
☎ 367-2710. Pizza with seafood.

Mangoes $-$$
Marsh Harbour
☎ 367-2366
Seafood, Bahamian and pizzas.

Man-O-War-Marina Pavilion $-$$
☎ 365-6185. Cold snacks and salads.

Mike's Bar and Restaurant $$
Green Turtle Cay
☎ 365-4219. Bahamian.

Mother Merle Fishnet $-$$
Dundas Town
☎ 367-2770. Famous for fried
chicken, conch fritters and other
Bahamian specialties.

Nettie's Museum Restaurant $$
Casuarina Point
☎ 366-2150. local fare.

Ole B's $-$$
Green Turtle Cay
Seafood and Bahamian snacks.

Pete's Pub and Gallery $$
Little Harbour
Seafood and Caribbean.

**Plymouth Rock Liquors
and Café** $-$$
Counter-style dining.

Point House Restaurant $$-$$$
Spanish Cay
☎ 365-0083
Seafood, Bahamian and European.

Reef Bar and Grill $-$$
Hope Town Harbour Lodge
☎ 366-0095
Seafood, Bahamian and Mexican.

Mangoes Restaurant Boutique $$
Marsh Harbour
☎ 367-2366

Rooster's Rest $-$$
New Plymouth
☎ 365-4066
Seafood, Bahamian and barbecue.

Rudy's Place $$-$$$
Gourmet Bahamian
☎ 366-0062
Great crawfish and Cornish game
hens, and excellent value set menu.

Sally's Take-Away $
Man-O-War-Cay
☎ 365-6240. Sandwiches and snacks.

Sand Dollar Café $
Great Guana Cay
Good value casual Bahamian lunches.

Sapodilly's $
Marsh Harbour
☎ 367-3498. Tasty Bahamian snacks.

Sea Spray Restaurant $$
White Sound, Elbow Cay
☎ 366-0045. Seafood and Bahamian.

Sea View Restaurant $-$$
New Plymouth
☎ 365-2007. Seafood and Bahamian.

Spanish Cay Inn $$
Spanish Cay
☎ 365-0083. Local and seafood.

Tiki Hut $-$$
Marsh Harbour
☎ 367-2575
Seafood and casual dining.

Wally's $$
Marsh Harbour
☎ 367-2074
Fine dining and live entertainment.

Wrecker's Bar $$
Spanish Cay
☎ 365-0083
Bahamian and Continental.

Wrecking Tree $$
New Plymouth
☎ 365-4263. Seafood and American.

Nightlife

Abaco Inn ☎ 366-0133

Harbour's Edge

Mike's Bar

Miss Emily's

Yahoes Sand Bar

Mangoes ☎ 367-2366

Sidi's Pub

Tiki Hut ☎ 367-2575

Wally's Club 404 ☎ 367-2074

Tipsy Seagull

Roosters Rest ☎ 365-4066

Captain Jack's

VISITS TO OUTLYING ISLANDS

The settlement makes a great base if you want to spend some time making day trips to outlying islands. One such trip is to picturesque Elbow Cay, which is easily accessible by boat. As you land there is a sign advising: 'Slow down, you're in Hope Town'. Hope Town is another very picturesque village with winding, narrow streets and clapboard and salt box houses and cottages, beautifully tended gardens bursting with bougainvillea and other exotic blooms. It has a fascinating small museum, the Wyannie Malone Museum, which traces the islands' history, including the wrecking era during the nineteenth century. The museum is in memory of Mrs. Malone who moved to the island in 1875, and many of her relatives still live there.

Wreckers

Islanders used to make a living by erecting lights so that passing ships, thinking they were approaching a port, would sail in to the shore where they would be wrecked on the reefs. The islanders would then salvage what they could from the broken ship. Wrecking was carried out at other locations on the islands, and it has been estimated that almost 500 ships foundered on the reefs, the result of natural or man-made disasters.

The best view of the small settlement is from the observation deck of the red and white candy striped 120ft (37m) tall lighthouse built in 1863, one of the last five in the world still hand-powered and fuelled by kerosene. And, it was not until the lighthouse was built that the wrecking industry ended. The town also has an art colony, and the nearby water offers good surfing.

Cherokee Sound, south of Marsh Harbour, is a small fishing community, and has some good wall dive sites in relatively shallow waters, while most of the other wall sites are in water too deep for sport divers. The Abaco Islands also have blue holes, some of which are connected by caves.

Just north of Marsh Harbour, you can visit **Man-O-War Cay**, the main boat-building area of The Bahamas, and also the model boat center. The shipwrights have also long used their skills to produce impressive, and often very intricate, model boats that are highly collectible. The island has a small, predominantly white population that welcomes visitors, but has resisted offers to build hotels and other attractions. Another quirk is that no alcohol is sold on the island. Offshore is the wreck of the Civil War vessel, the *Adirondack* lying in 30ft (9m) of water offshore. It sank in 1862 and some of her cannon are still visible. It is a popular dive site because of the number of different corals and wide variety of fish life.

Most of the main settlements are on the east side of Great Abaco, the main island that is protected by offshore reefs and cays. It is a great place to stroll around as the lanes are quiet, and local women still stroll along them skillfully balancing trays of fruit and vegetables on their heads. You can visit the settlements of **Cooper's town** and **Cedar Harbour.** The small **Albert Bootle Museum** at the Government Dock, Cooper's Town, depicts island life and history.

There are dense forests of tropical pines, and wild boar still roam in them. They are hunted down for special occasions, and sometimes feature on hotel menus at festival time. There are also a number of wild horses.

There are, however, resorts on Walker's, Green Turtle, Spanish Cay and Treasure Cays, when you get to enjoy all the facilities the international holidaymaker expects. **Treasure Cay** has a fine resort, a championship golf course and hosts two annual fishing tournaments, the Treasure Cay Billfish Tournament in April, and the Treasure Cay Invitational each May. Treasure Cay, which is a narrow peninsula and not really an island, also boasts a stunning 3-mile (5km) long beach, and a golf course designed by Dick Wilson. **Green Turtle Cay**, is 2 miles (3km) off the mainland, and has a number of picturesque, brightly painted old houses and fine beaches, and **Great Guana Cay** is also popular because of its 7-mile (11km) long sugar sand beach. At Carlton Point,

settlers from North America still loyal to the British Crown established the first settlement on Abaco in 1783.

And, if you then feel like a little peace and quiet, you can hire a boat for a few days and explore the adjacent islands. The beaches on **Elbow Cay, Great Guana and Manjack Cay** are considered to be among the best in The Bahamas. Although there is a lot of land to explore with wonderful beaches and secluded coves, The Abaco Islands particularly appeal to boaters.

Good diving

Pelican Cays Land & Sea Park has long been a popular area for divers with wonderfully bright corals, especially purple seafan, brain coral and elkhorn. The park covers an area of 2,100 acres (840 hectares) and the reefs support a wealth of marine life, including grouper, ray, barracuda, tarpon and nurse shark, as well as octopus, huge lobsters and turtles. There is also an extensive cavern and tunnel complex to explore which plays host to huge shoals of multi-shaded fish, such as the dazzling silverside minnow and yellowtail snappers.

Fowl Cay Land and Sea Preserve takes in the reef, which is only a few minutes ride from Marsh Harbour. There are coral mountains and caves and it is a great place for novice divers because of the large number of shallow dive sites.

Hole-In-The-Wall is at the southeastern tip of Great Abaco, and has been formed over centuries by wind and sea erosion. Above it stands a navigational lighthouse, and in the nearby waters are a number of ocean holes, many of which have not been fully explored. North of Hole-In-The-Wall is **Sandy Point**, a pretty fishing village with lovely beach that is popular with shell collectors.

Gorda Cay covers 1,000 acres (400 hectares) and was acquired by Disney Cruise Lines in 1996 after a yearlong search for 'an island paradise'. The island is used for daylong stops for the cruise lines two ships.

THE ANDROS ISLANDS

This is the largest but least explored island chain in the group covering 2,300sq miles (5983sq km). They have a population of 8180, are known as the Bonefishing Capital of the World, and include North Andros, Central Andros and South Andros.

Travelling around the Andros Islands

The islands are 104 miles (167km) long and 40 miles (64km) wide, and are connected by a series of channels, known as bights. There are four main towns, Nicoll's Town in the north, Andros Town and Mangrove Cay in the middle, and Congo Town in the south. All can be reached by plane or boat and there are regular services from Nassau. There is an airport at San Andros in the north, at Andros Town and Mangrove Cay in the middle of the chain, and at Congo Town in the south. There are ports of entry at Fresh Creek near Andros Town, Mastic Point close to San Andros, and Congo Town. Mail boats from Nassau also visit a number of the islands' coastal communities.

Nicoll's Town, Andros Beach

Collecting water from a well in Andros

Mythical creatures of the forest

The dense forests of Andros also provided a refuge for runaway slaves for almost two centuries, and these forests were also the home of the mischievous chickcharnies, which feature so prominently in Andros folklore. The chickcharnies are strange looking bearded gremlins that hang from trees and bestow good luck or bad luck on passers-by depending on what sort of mind they are in. These mythical creatures feature prominently in Bahamian folklore, especially on Andros, and should be easy to spot because they are supposed to have only three fingers and three toes, piercing red eyes, and they hang upside down from the branches. If they like the look of you they can bring you good luck, but if they don't, watch out!

The island has a range of accommodation from small guest houses to grand resorts and marinas, but because of its size, there are large unpopulated areas, and a great deal to see and do, both on land and in the water. In fact, water is one of the main resources of the island because there are large underground reserves of pure drinking water. Barges regularly arrive at the island to fill up with water that is then taken to Nassau where it boosts the local drinking water supplies.

The first Spanish visitors called the island La Isla del Espiritu (Island of the Holy Spirit) because it was so beautiful and had so much fresh water. It was thought that the Holy Spirit was at its most powerful over water. There were many Loyalist plantations on the island and traces of many of the old logging trails can still be found.

The main settlement is **Nicholl's Town**, the island's largest village, and situated on the north-east coast. It has shops, telephone office, clinic, small hotels and restaurants. About 5 miles (8km) north is **Morgan's Beach**. Henry Morgan, the Welsh buccaneer, who was later knighted and became Deputy Governor of Jamaica, is said to have buried part of his fabulous treasure in one of the caves off nearby **Morgan's Bluff**.

Andros Town is on the eastern coast and nearby **Fresh Creek**, is a popular diving area. Inland is **Captain Bill's Blue Hole**, a large freshwater spring. There are many paths around Andros Town through the forests, and there is a huge variety of flora, from island herbs and spices, rare orchids to magnificent flowering tropical plants. Many of the plants have healing properties and have been used by the islanders for centuries as bush medicine.

The village of **Red Bays** is famous for its basket weavers, and the descendants of Seminole Indians who fled from the Florida Everglades in the mid-nineteenth century, and settled here. They still have their own culture and traditions, and are probably responsible for the chickcharnies legend.

Andros also boasts the third largest barrier reef in the world, and the second largest in the western hemisphere, and offers spectacular diving. One of the most popular dive sites is the Tongue of the Ocean, where the reef plunges to a depth of 6,000ft (1830m). It is such a spectacular plunge, that both the US and British Royal Navy have used it to test submarines. Another extraordinary feature to be found around the island is the offshore Blue Holes, which is very popular with divers.

There are also many caverns, tunnels and chimneys to explore. Other dive sites include *The Barge* that lies in about 70ft (21m) of water in Fresh Creek. It was a landing craft deliberately sunk to create an artificial reef. There is also the Fresh Creek wall covered with black coral which drops from about 80ft (24m) to 180ft (55m), and a blue hole which attracts rays and sharks because of the teeming fish life.

The reefs around the islands have also been responsible for many shipwrecks over the centuries. Two of the wreck sites that can be dived over are *The Lady Gloria* and *The Potomac*. Local dive operators arrange wreck dive tours.

And, like its adjacent islands, Andros is rightly famous for its world-class fishing, especially for marlin and bluefin tuna. The bonefishing attracts the world's best anglers.

There is much to see and do on land as well. The northern area is known as **The Big Yard**, and is largely covered with dense forest of mahogany and pine. There are more than 50 varieties of orchid, many of them tiny and several of them very rare. The west coast is marshland, referred to locally as **The Mud**, while the east coast has quiet

Mysterious Blue Holes

The origin of these deep cauldrons of warm, clear water is still not known for certain, but it is thought that millions of years ago, an area of land around the island must also have been above water level. Rainwater permeated through the limestone rocks eating out huge underground caves, then at some point, the water level rose and these caverns disappeared under the sea. Erosion continued, however, but this time, instead of enlarging the caves, the action of the sea water steadily wore away at the roof of the cave until it collapsed, forming the deep pools. There are a number of blue holes, many of which have been named such as Benjamin's, Cousteau's, Uncle Charley's blue hole and so on. The exact number of blue holes is not known, and new ones continue to be discovered.

beaches protected by the 120-mile (193km) long barrier reef.

There is another large area of dense forest and mangrove swamp in the south of the island. The area covers 40sq miles (104sq km) and is a naturalist's dream. You can spot the white crowned pigeon, whistling duck, herons and egrets, many species of butterflies, as well as lizards and snakes, including the Bahamian boa constrictor. None of the snakes on The Bahamas are poisonous, but there are many myths surrounding the boa constrictor, which is known locally as the fowl snake, because of its preferred diet.

You can also watch the fascinating West Indian flamingo, The Bahamas national bird, during migrations. These are not the Bahamas flamingo, but mostly migrants on passage to and from Cuba. Other spectacular sights include the late spring and summer migration of the huge Andros land crab from the forest to the sea, and the giant iguanas, which can grow to 6ft (2m) in length. As you wander through the forest, look out for the chickcharnies.

EATING OUT & NIGHTLIFE

• Andros Islands •

Aquamarine $$
Calabash Bay
☎ 368-2064. Island and seafood.

The Beacon $$
Andros Lighthouse Yacht Club
☎ 368-2305
Seafood and Bahamian dishes.

Big Josh Seafood Restaurant $-$$
Lowe Sound
☎ 329-2517. Seafood.

Emerald Palms By The Sea $$
☎ 369-2661
Seafood and Bahamian fare.

Flamingo Club $$
Drigg's hill, ☎ 326-4671
Seafood and local specialties.

Golden Conch $$
Fresh Creek
☎ 368-2064. Island and seafood.

Kemp's $$
Fresh Creek
☎ 369-3796. Island and seafood.

Morgan's Treasure $$
Morgan's Bluff
☎ 329-2072. Island fare and seafood.

Small Hope Bay Lodge $$
☎ 368-2013
Bahamian and American.

Square Deal $$
Mangrove Cay
☎ 369-0161
Steaks, seafood and island dishes.

Nightlife

Mal Jack's and Blue Bird Club
South Andros

Donnie's Sweet Sugar Lounge
Fresh Creek
☎ 368-2080

Leadon's
Behring Point
☎ 368-4167

Roger Munning's Night Club
Mastic Point

Sugar Shack
Nicholl's Town
☎ 329-2194

THE BERRY ISLANDS

The Berry Islands cover 30 small islands, scores of tiny cays, and an area of 12sq miles (31sq km). They are a mecca for diving, yachting, bird watching and sport fishing, and have a population of about 700. Most people live on Great Harbour Cay with its beautiful white-sand beaches fringed by palm and pines. The waters offer excellent diving. The islands are on the eastern edge of the Great Bahama Bank and below the surface there are reefs and strange rock formations, and the wrecks of ships that have foundered there. Private charters service the Berry Islands that have airstrips on Chub Cay and Great Harbour Cay. There is also a regular boat service between the islands and Nassau. Bullock's Harbour is the main village with stores and some restaurants. The main resort is the Great Harbour Cay resort that has a marina, golf course and privately owned villas and town houses that are let when the owners are not using them.

BIMINI ISLANDS

The Bimini Islands, covering 9sq miles (23sq km) are the closest to Florida and just 50 miles (80km) off the southeast mainland coast. The two islands of North and South Bimini are regarded by many as the 'big game fishing capital of the world', and were the setting for Ernest Hemingway's novel *Islands in the Stream*. The two islands, separated by a narrow channel, have a combined population of 1600, and a rich history. There is an airport on South Bimini, but most visitors arrive in the North Bimini Harbour on the seaplane from Miami, Fort Lauderdale and Paradise Island, a 20-minute ride away. There are ports of entry at Alice Town and Cat Cay, and regular boat services between the islands and Nassau.

Baily Town on North Bimini is the main population center, on the Queen's Highway that, with the King's Highway, are the two main roads on the island. The village has a hodge-podge of brightly painted homes, Roman Catholic Church and the Methodist Church, built in 1858 complete with bell tower. There are about another 10 churches on the island.

Alice Town, also on North Bimini, is the main resort area with hotels, restaurants, a bank and charter boats. There are also the small settlements of **Porgy Bay** and **Bimini Bay**. Bimini bread is an island specialty, and is delicious straight from the oven. A few of the islanders still use clay outdoor Dutch ovens for some of their cooking.

History of the Bimini Islands

The history of The Bimini Islands is fascinating and steeped in legend. There are stories that the islands are part of the Lost Continent of Atlantis, and that Ponce de Leon landed during his search for the Fountain of Youth, and found it on the islands. Locals will point out the spring which they claim is the mystical fountain, but almost every island in the northern Caribbean has at least one site which they insist is the real one.

The Bimini Islands are, perhaps, the best known of the Out Islands because of their world-class sport fishing, which has been given added publicity by such celebrities as writers Zane Grey and Hemingway. Hemingway landed a 513lb (233kg) tuna here and a huge blue marlin, which has become the subject of many legends. The Bimini Islands are also popular with yachtsmen and divers, but most people do come to fish.

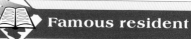

Famous resident

Ernest Hemingway lived on the island between 1931 and 1937, and used to spend months at a time fishing here, as did Adam Clayton Powell Jr, another avid American fisherman. Hemingway is said to have spent much of his time when not fishing, drinking in The Compleat Angler (☎ 346-3122) a lively hotel bar in the main settlement of Alice Town, which has an interesting collection of Hemingway memorabilia in the small **Hemingway Museum** off the lobby. A sign by the hotel proclaims you are now at 'The Gateway to The Bahamas'. And when Hemingway was not fishing or drinking, he was writing at **Marlin Cottage,** which is now part of the **Bimini Blue Water Resort**, and can be rented (☎ 347-3166).

New York Congressman Adam Clayton Powell Jr reportedly divided his time equally between fishing and drinking, but he frequented the tiny End of the World Bar in Alice Town. The bar has been described as 'slightly larger than a garden tool shed with a loose sandy floor.'

Hemingway has an annual fishing tournament named after him, the Hemingway Championship in March.

In the shallow inshore waters, especially close to Alice Town where the seaplanes land, there is excellent bone fishing. Further out there is big game fishing for dolphin, tuna, amberjack, white and blue marlin, swordfish, barracuda, grouper, several members of the shark family and many other species. The money that game fishing brings in has been vital in the development of the islands, so much so, that the marlin features on the B$100, the country's highest bank note. As part of a major conservation effort, the Bahamian government has launched a tag-and-release scheme, and this has provided valuable research data about the migration, age and growth patterns of these game fish.

The islands host a number of major fishing tournaments each year, which attract world-class anglers because some of the world's biggest fish have been caught here. More than 40 fishing tournaments are sponsored each year by The Bahamas Ministry of Tourism, Sports and Aviation Department (perhaps responsible for flying fish!), and among the most important are the billfish tournament in June, and the wahoo tournament in November. The fishing tournament season gets under way each year in March with the Bacardi Tournament.

Boating and fishing arrangements can be made through The Big Game Fishing Club and Hotel, Bimini Blue Water, The Compleat Angler Hotel, Sea Crest Hotel and Marina, All My Children Hotel and Weech's Bimini Dock. All offer guided trips, fishing charters and boats for hire, either bare boat or crewed.

The waters around The Bimini Islands are near perfect for scuba diving with excellent visibility, lots of good dive sites, and some incredible drop-offs, one plunging more than 2000ft (915m). Divers can explore 'trees' of black coral over **The Bimini Wall**, or enjoy the teeming fish life around the **Victory Rocks**, the 4 miles (6km) of reefs and coral canyons off Victory Cay. The *Bimini Barge* lies in 90ft (27m) of water, and the *Bimini Trader*, a casualty of Hurricane Andrew that tore through the region in August 1992, lies in 85ft (26m) of water. You can try to count how many different species of fish there are at **Little Caverns**, and try to explain the **Bimini Road**, huge slabs of stone which lie in 15ft (5m) of water, and which some claim to be part of the Lost City of Atlantis. Other areas worth exploring are **Rainbow** and **Hawksbill Reefs**.

Bimini Undersea Adventures offers a comprehensive list of facilities, including diving instruction, certification, equipment hire and diving trips, and Brown's Hotel also offers diving. The **Concrete Ship** is the wreck of the *Sapona*, which was built during World War I, was used in the 1920s to run rum to the US during Prohibition, and as a bombing target during World War II.

About 8 miles (11km) south is exclusive **Cat Cay**, not to be confused with Cat Island. You can visit the island, which has its own private airstrip, but are not allowed to overnight unless a guest at the club or marina.

CAT ISLAND

The island covers 150sq miles (390sq km) and has a population of 1698. It is the sixth largest island in The Bahamas, and should not be confused with Cat Cay that is near the Bimini Islands. It was probably named after Captain Arthur Catt, a British privateer, and has a very untypical Bahamian landscape with lush green forests and rolling hills, surrounded by cliffs and pristine beaches. It also boasts the highest point in The Bahamas with Mount Alvernia at 206ft (63m), where Father Jerome hand-built the Hermitage. The island is noted for its miles of deserted beaches, including an 8 mile (13km) long pink sand beach, and it was the boyhood home of actor Sidney Poitier who grew up in Arthur's Town.

There are flights from Nassau to Arthur's Town Airport and New Bight, and charters from Florida and Nassau into New Bight and Hawk's Nest. Mail boats also serve the island from Nassau.

Arthur's Town is the main settlement at the northern end of the island with an airport and some shops. Most of the population, as with the other villages along the coast, is engaged in fishing. **Bennett's Harbour** to the north was one of the first villages on the island and has many old cottages with their outdoor rock ovens.

The Bight has a fabulous beach and the two small settlements of **New Bight** and **Old Bight** in the north. You can visit the remains of **Pigeon Bay Cottage**, a former nineteenth-century estate house. **Columbus Point** is at the south-east tip of the island, although whether it had any association with the explorer is not known.

The **Deveaux Plantation Ruins**, in the south of the island, are all that remains of a Great House of a cotton plantation owned by Colonel Andrew Deveaux. He is famous for having led the raid on Nassau in 1783 when the English re-took the capital from the Spanish occupiers. As a reward, the English crown gave him a land grant covering much of Cat Island. Today, the shell of the building is overrun by lush tropical vegetation.

Devil's Point on the south coast west of Cutlass Bay, seems an unfortunate name for a village that is very picturesque with its old, weather-beaten gaily painted and thatched Loyalist cottages. There are more remains of old plantations near the village. **Fernandez Bay Village** is near the foot of Mt. Alvernia on a sweeping bay that offers great inshore snorkeling from the beach. **Hawk's Nest Creek** on the south-west coast and has a large heronry

Port Howe has a somewhat infamous past and was one of the main wrecking areas in the seventeenth and eighteenth centuries, when

The Hermitage and Mount Alvernia Stations of the Cross

The **Hermitage** is a hand-built mini-monastery, built in the 1940s by Father Jerome, born as John Hawes. Although born an Anglican he later converted to Catholicism, which explains why there are both Anglican and Catholic churches in The Bahamas built by him before moving to Cat Island where he lived as a recluse in the hermitage. There is a winding path along which the 14 Stations of the Cross are carved. Father Jerome hand carved the steps in the rock to create the path up the mountain and was also responsible for creating the Stations of the Cross. He spent the last years of his life on the island, and died in 1956 aged 80. He is buried in a tomb on top of the mountain, which is regarded by many as a shrine.

lights would be lit on nearby Columbus Point to trick ships into turning landward on to the reefs.

The Cat Island terrapin is only found on this island, which also offers excellent birding. The beaches are popular with turtles who haul themselves up the sand to lay their eggs, and whales and dolphins can sometimes been seen offshore.

Berry Islands Bimini Islands and Cat Island

Berry Islands

Backside Inn $-$$
Great Harbour Cay
Light snacks, and nightly dancing.

Coolie Mae's Take-Away $
Great Harbour Cay
Bahamian dishes.

Flying Bridge $$
Chub Cay
☎ 325-1490
Bahamian and American.

Mama and Papa T's Beach Club $
Great Harbour Cay
Snacks and sandwiches.

Tamboo Dinner Club $$
Great Harbour Cay
☎ 367-8302. Seafood and American.

Watergate Chicken Shack $$
Great Harbour Cay
Chicken and fish snacks.

Wharf Restaurant and Bar $$
Great Harbour Cay marina
Seafood, Bahamian and American.

Bimini Islands

Anchorage $$-$$$
Bimini Blue Water Resort
☎ 347-3166
Seafood and international.

Bahamian Kitchen $$
☎ 347-3391
Seafood and authentic Bahamian.

CJ's Deli $
☎ 347-2171
Fine dining and afternoon tea.

Big John's $$
Alice Town
☎ 347-3166. Local.

**Bimini Big Game Club
and Hotel** $$-$$$
Alice Town
☎ 347-3391
Excellent Bahamian and American
cuisine.

Bimini Blue Water Resort $$-$$$
☎ 347-3166. The Anchorage Restaurant is noted for its fresh seafood
and steaks. Try the stuffed lobster or
lobster salad. Among the best food
on the island and great sunsets.

Captain Bob's $-$$
Alice Town
☎ 347-3260. Bahamian dishes.

Compleat Angler $$
☎ 347-2122. Live entertainment.

Cortiz Deli $-$$
Alice Town
☎347-2187.

Diandrea's Deli $-$$
Alice Town
☎ 347-3334.

Fisherman's Paradise $-$$
Alice Town
☎ 347-3220.

Fisherman's Wharf $$
☎ 347-2391. Seafood and American.

Red Lion Pub $$
Alice Town
☎ 347-3259
Seafood, steaks and American.

Sandra's $$
Bailey Town
☎347-2336. Local.

South Bimini Yacht Club $$
South Bimini
☎ 347-3115. Local and international.

Nightlife
Admiral Hotel
Bailey Town, ☎ 347-2347.

Bimini Big Game Club
☎ 347-3391.

Bimini Breeze
Alice Town, ☎ 347-3511.

Blue Marlin Restaurant
Alice Town, ☎ 347-3374.

Conchman's Bar
Alice Town ☎347-3449.

Seaview Disco
Alice Town ☎347-3220.

All My Children Disco
Alice Town ☎347-3334.

Compleat Angler
☎ 347-2122.

Cat Island
Batchelor's Rest $$
☎ 342-6014. Fine dining.

Bridge Inn Restaurant $$
New Bight
☎ 342-3013
International and Bahamian.

Fernandez Bay Village $$
☎ 342-3043. Buffet beach dinner,
reservations required.

Greenwood Beach Resort $$
☎ 342-3053
Bahamian and Continental.

Hawk's Nest Resort $$
Hawk's Nest
☎ 357-7257
International and seafood.

Peter Hill Restaurant $$
Old Bight
☎ 342-4001. Bahamian and seafood.

Sea Spray Hotel $$
Orange Creek
☎ 354-4116. Seafood, Bahamian and
International.

CROOKED ISLAND AND ACKLINS ISLAND

Remote Crooked Island covers 92sq miles (239sq km), and has miles of deserted, sand beaches, large areas of tidal flats and deep creeks offering excellent fishing for tarpon and bonefish, and undisturbed pristine reefs. The earliest settlers were Loyalists from the newly independent American States, who brought their slaves with them and established cotton plantations. The cotton industry did not last, but many of the island's residents are descended from those slaves, and they still farm the land. The 400 plus population live in small, delightful fishing villages. One feature of the island is the fragrance from herbs and wild flowers that fill the air, giving it the local name of 'The Fragrant Isle'.

There are scheduled and charter flights into Colonel Hill airport on Crooked Island and Sprint Point on Acklins.

Crooked Island is separated from **Acklins Island** by the Crooked Island Passage that was one of the routes used most frequently by galleons sailing between the Old World and the New. Some experts believe that Columbus landed on Crooked Island although this is a matter of hot debate.

Offshore there are coral gardens to be explored, with spectacular drop-offs and reefs for divers. The waters shelve gently from 6ft (2m) to about 40ft (12m), and then plummet to 3600ft (1100m) in the Crooked Island Passage.

The white Bird Rock lighthouse was built in 1878 to protect the northern Crooked Island Passage, and it is still operating, while in the south there is the **Castle Island** light. There are caves around the south of island that were used by pirates, thus the name **Pirates Bluff**. Many of these caves are now home to large colonies of bats. Flamingos do not nest on the island, but they can often be seen feeding on Crooked Island. Other unusual wildlife to be seen include rock iguanas, hutias and white crowned pigeons.

The ruins of the oldest post office in The Bahamas, and the first in the Western Hemisphere, now the dining room and pub at **Pittstown Point Landings**, are there. Also of interest are the ruins of **Marine Farm**, possibly built originally as a fortification because Spanish armaments were discovered there; and the remains of **Hope Great House**, surrounded by gardens and fruit trees. The Bahamas National Trust administers both of these sites.

DEEP WATER CAY

This remote private island is 125 miles (201 km) due east of Palm Beach, and off the east coast of Grand Bahama. It covers only 80 acres (32 hectares), but is set in 250sq miles (650sq km) of shallows, flats and creeks offering outstanding fishing, and world-class trophy bone fishing. There are shallow reefs and drop-offs for snorkelers and scuba divers, and more than 300 species of bird have been recorded.

ELEUTHERA

It covers 200sq miles (520sq km) and includes the main island of Eleuthera, plus Cupid's Cay, Spanish Wells and Harbour Island. They have a population of about 10,600, making them one of the most populated of the out island groups, and are noted for their fabulous pink sand beaches. Eleuthera is 110 miles (177km) long, making it one of the longest islands in The Bahamas, although it is rarely more than 2 miles (3km) wide. It does boast, however, more than 300 miles (480 km) of coastline that includes miles of beautiful beaches, secluded coves, cliffs and offshore reefs.

Inland there are gently, rolling hills. The main settlements in the north are Current, Gregory Town and Hatchet Bay and a road then runs the length of the island to the southern tip, a two hour drive away through pineapple groves and the rich farmland. The island is about 60 miles (100km) west of Nassau, and the fact that it has three airports at North Eleuthera, Governor's Harbour and Rock Sound – shows how popular it is with the jet set. There are ports of entry at Cape Eleuthera, Governor's Harbour, Harbour Island, Hatchet Bay, North Eleuthera and Rock Sound.

While the islands play host to the rich and famous, they also make an ideal holiday destination for the budget-conscious, with a wide range of accommodation. Because of the length of the island, it is a good idea to make sure you are flying in to the most appropriate airport. There are daily flights from Nassau, Miami and Fort Lauderdale, and there is also the mail boat that plies between Nassau and Eleuthera's many ports.

Eleuthera's history

The island was first settled by Lucayan Indians, Amerindians from South America, who were skilled canoe and boat builders, and who had traveled northwards through the Caribbean. They were mostly farmers and fishermen.

The first European settlers were English dissidents from Bermuda who were seeking a settlement where they could worship in freedom. They chose the name Eleuthera because it is the Greek word for 'freedom'. They arrived in 1648 aboard two ships, one of which foundered on Devil's Backbone, a reef just off the northernmost point of the island. The survivors struggled ashore and took shelter in what is now known as Preacher's Cave.

The Eleutheran Adventurers split into two groups and established settlements on Current Island, just offshore from the mainland, and at Cupid's Cay, which at that time could be reached from the mainland at low tide. A bridge built to connect the two was blown away during a 1929 hurricane, and later replaced by the causeway that now provides easy access.

While their dream settlements did not survive for long, the islands today have a remarkably peaceful air about them, with pretty, pastel-painted homes, picket fences and well tended gardens. The waters surrounding the islands are equally calm because of the protective reefs, and are noted for their brilliant blue. There are scores of secluded sandy beaches, and the island is really a handful of communities separated from one another by miles of wonderful sandy beaches.

Offshore, there is excellent diving and snorkeling, and the reefs can easily be reached from the beaches. Regatta sailing is almost a national pastime in The Bahamas, and Eleuthera hosts three major events each year, drawing large numbers of competitors, many sailing locally-built sloops. The main regattas are the North Eleuthera Regatta held in October, the All Eleuthera Regatta held in early August in Governor's Harbour, and the South Eleuthera Homecoming in March. There are marinas at the Cotton Bay Club, Harbour Island Club and Marina Harbour Club, Harbour Island Town Dock, Spanish Wells Marina, Spanish Wells Yacht Haven and Valentine's Yacht Club and Inn.

Preacher's Cave in North Eleuthera, gets its name because the first settlers sheltered here and made a stone altar to celebrate their first religious service. Another large boulder at the end of the cave is believed to have been the pulpit.

In 1992 the Spanish Wells Museum conducted an archaeological dig in the cave which unearthed some artifacts and the remains of two bodies, one a woman and the other a young child, both wrapped in cloth held together by brass pins, and believed to have been buried between the mid-seventeenth century and the early eighteenth century. Pieces of clay pipes, some bearing the English maker's name, were found, together with utensils and crockery. The beaches around the cave are beautiful and popular with both islanders and visitors. The cave is open to the public.

Also close to the cave on the north west coast is **The Bluff**, a small and old farming community, growing mostly citrus, and some docking facilities. The community has traditionally produced excellent weavers who today make straw baskets and tourist souvenirs.

About 5 miles (8km) along the coast from The Bluff, are the two communities of **Upper and Lower Bogue**. Lower Bogue is the larger of the two and just to the north. Both are farming communities and their name is a derivation of the word Bog, because much of the surrounding countryside is swampy. There are restaurants and bars.

Natural wonder

The **Glass Window Bridge** is the narrowest point of the island, just 30ft (9m) across. The natural bridge connects the two sections of the island, and separates the blue waters of the Atlantic and the turquoise waters of the bay. The land immediately to the north and south is about 85ft (26m) above sea level, but plummets in a cliff to the narrow bridge. There used to be a top arch, but this was washed away a long time ago. Apart from the unusual rock formations, the most spectacular sight is the different colors on either side of the bridge. It inspired artist Winslow Homer to capture the scene on canvas in 1885 and the painting now hangs in a New York Museum.

Eleuthera

The two main settlements of **Spanish Wells** and **Harbour Island** are reached off the northern tip of Eleuthera. Spanish Wells gets its name because sailors used to stop here to dig wells for water. The drinking water could be drawn from not far below the surface, and the sailors would collect it in barrels to provide them with drinking supplies on their trans-Atlantic crossing back to Spain. The people have made their living from the sea for the last 300 years, and today the community is booming thanks to the successful crawfish business. The islanders are also excellent fishermen, fishing guides and pilots.

HARBOUR ISLAND

Tiny Harbour Island off Eleuthera's north coast is the home of the famous pink beaches. The locals call it Briland and it has long been noted because of the skill of its shipwrights. In 1783 the local farmers were given a land grant to farm on Eleuthera because it had more fertile soil, and this is still carried on.

The island is 3 miles (5km) long and half a mile (0.8km) wide, and the sand gets its pink tinge from crushed coral and shells. The island boasts a number of resorts from very exclusive to relatively economic. The pink beaches run almost the length of the east coast and the waters, protected by offshore reefs, offer safe swimming. The island is one mile (1.6km) off the coast of North Eleuthera and can only be reached by water ferry.

It is also famous for the historic settlement of **Dunmore Town**, the original capital of The Bahamas. Dunmore Town is named after Lord Dunmore, a former Governor of Virginia, and has wonderful gaily painted, old clapboard houses with their white lattice work, shuttered windows, balconies and immaculately tended flower gardens. During the late eighteenth century the town developed ship-building and sugar refining, and this in turn led to rum distillation.

You can stroll down the original narrow streets past the outdoor cafés; enjoy fresh fruit from one of the many street vendors. Along Bay Street you can buy the island's famous batik clothing, and you can take **Hill Steps** that were hand hewn out of the rock by prisoners. **Titus Hole**, close to the waterfront, is said to have been the island's first prison.

There are also many pleasant walks on the island that offer the chance to see the diverse plant life, such as fig and casuarina pine, and spectacular sea views, as well as strolls along the sand to watch the stunning sunsets. The two famous marinas attract yachtsmen from around the world. St. John's Anglican Church and the Wesley Methodist Church are two of the oldest in The Bahamas, both built in the mid-eighteenth century.

There are dive shops at the **Romora Bay Club** and **Valentine's Yacht Club**, and many excellent dive sites. Among the best are the **Devil's Backbone**, which is littered with the wrecks of ships – and even an old locomotive engine that fell from a barge in 1865. It was part of a Union train captured by the Confederacy and it was being shipped to Cuba where it had been sold to a sugar plantation. **The Plateau** is noted because of the rich marine life and the many species of fish that can be seen.

BACK TO ELEUTHERA

Further south is **Gregory Town**, the pineapple capital of the islands, and named after John Gregory, a former Governor of The Bahamas. The people take great pride in the appearance of their community and the prettily painted cottages and red tiled villas hug the hillside that slopes down to the water. The tiny **St. Gregory's Catholic Church** is worth a visit. The local beaches offer excellent surfing, and nearby **Surfers Beach**, about 2 miles (3km) away, is not only one of the finest surfing spots in The Bahamas, it has been rated by experts as one of the best surfing beaches in the world.

Pineapple capital

Every March in Gregory Town, the Pineapple Arts Festival takes place and provides islanders with the chance to display their music, crafts and paintings, and at the beginning of June, the Pineapple Festival takes place. It is a four-day fair and one of the highlights is a pineapple recipe contest. You can see the pineapples growing quite close to the roads, and pineapple rum is a local specialty. The pineapples are harvested twice a year, during the summer and the winter, and while both are delicious, the summer fruit are sweeter because of greater sunshine.

Hatchet Bay once a prosperous plantation, and **Ten Bay Caves** are about five miles (8km) south of Gregory Town. The quay in its narrow mouth, is so sheltered it is said to be hurricane proof. Hatchet Bay used to be called East End Point, but was renamed because the bay resembles the shape of an axe.

The major attraction is **The Cave**, at the end of a long, dusty red earth track. The entrance is a small hole, not much larger than a doorway, and the path then slopes quite steeply down to the first cavern, which is almost 100ft (30m) in diameter, but with a low ceiling. Flickering lights cast eerie shadows. Steps have been carved into the rock to allow the islanders to gather guano, the droppings of huge colonies of bats, which was used on the fields as fertilizer. The Cave extends for about a mile (1.6km) with a number of caverns carved from the limestone and coral with fantastic shapes and great stalagmites and stalactites (stalactites hang down so have to hang on 'tite' so they don't fall off). There are also pools, both freshwater from permeating rain, and salt water.

On the eastern side of the bay is the small farming town of **Alice Town** with its tree lined streets and gaily painted houses and well-tended flower gardens. About 2 miles (3km) away on the Atlantic coast is the **Shark Hole**. A poultry plant slaughters about 8,000 chickens a day and the offal has traditionally been dumped into the Shark Hole, which has been carved into the cliff by the seas. The offal is then washed out to sea on the tide, but while the dumping takes place, a crowd normally gathers and some islanders throw buoyed lines into the water to try to catch fish that are attracted to the bloody water. Sharks are frequently caught.

Rainbow Bay gets its name from the spectacular shades that flash across the rocks and sea as the sun sets, and it offers excellent snorkeling. Next is **James Cistern**, a small fishing village built on the hillside. As you head south, you pass the former United States Air

Roadside food

On the Out Islands as elsewhere, many of the homes have outside clay ovens which are used daily to bake the most delicious breads. There are often roadside stalls selling tasty Bahamian fast food such as barbecued chicken, rice'n peas, and even piping hot macaroni cheese, straight from the oven.

Force missile tracking station, and a navy base, and then you run into Governor's Harbour in the middle of the island.

Governor's Harbour was the site of the earliest settlement in The Bahamas, and was named because it was the seat of Government under Captain William Sayle. Today, it is the island's administrative area and the seat of local government, with a range of accommodation. The international airport is a 15-minute drive away. The town, with its many fine old homes, nestles at the foot of poinciana draped hills beside the large, sheltered port where the mail boats dock, and across the bay, connected by a causeway, is tiny **Cupid's Cay**, the site of the first Eleutheran settlement in The Bahamas. The tiny St. Patrick's Anglican Church in Governor's Harbour celebrated its centenary in 1992.

The small, sprawling communities of **North and South Palmetto Point**, are mostly engaged in agriculture. The private resort on the east coast

A beautiful 110 year old Anglican church, Governor's Harbour

of **Windermere Island** which attracted the rich, royal and famous, has closed but you can still land on the island and enjoy the beaches.

Rock Sound in the south is now the largest community on the island. It used to be called Wreck Sound, because the islanders would erect lights to trick ships into thinking there was a port. The ships would sail towards the lights and founder on the rocks where their cargoes could be salvaged. The Rock Sound International Airport is nearby. The main road, Front Street runs along the coast with its pretty cottages one side, and fishing boats pulled up on to the beach on the other. The white St. Luke's Lutheran Church looks out over the sea.

Just north of town is **Tarpum Bay**, a lovely fishing village with a small artist community where you can view the works of US artist Mal Flanders. Many of the people living in Tarpum Bay earn their living from the sea, fishing or running charter boats to the fish rich waters of the Schooner Cays, a few miles to the south. The area around Tarpum Bay has many fine, deserted beaches.

The **Cotton Bay Club** that was developed as a retreat for millionaires, in 450 acres (180 hectares) of immaculately landscaped gardens with secluded pink shuttered cottages and an 18 hole par-72 Robert Trent Jones golf course, is now closed although the golf course is open. There is a bridge over Rock Sound to Windermere Island, which was a favorite holiday spot of Prince Charles and Princess Diana There are many private villas belonging to the rich and famous.

There are a number of small farming and fishing communities scattered through the south of the island, such as Green Castle, Wemyss Bight and Bannerman Town, on the southern tip with the Bannerman Town Lighthouse.

There are snorkeling opportunities all round the islands, but especially in the protected **Cove Eleuthera** that teems with fish life. One of the best dives is at **Current Cut**, so called because divers have to contend with a 5-knot drift. Large schools of spotted eagle rays and horse-eye Jacks are regularly seen here.

Bottomless lake

Rock Sound has a number of interesting sights, including the **Ocean Hole**, a large inland lake about 120yd (110m) in diameter, connected to the sea by tunnels. Legend has it that the lake at Rock Sound, is bottomless, and it certainly is very deep. It is said that tropical fish swim through the tunnels from the sea into the lake, and steps have been cut into the coral so that visitors can walk down to the water and feed the fish, mostly parrot and rainbow fish, by hand. It is a great place to swim and take photographs. There is an another hole, about 250ft (76m) across, to the east of Rock Sound but it is best to ask an islander to guide you there.

Eleuthera

The Blue Room $$
Governor's Harbour
☎ 332-2736. Seafood and Bahamian.

Buccaneer Club $$
Governor's Harbour
☎ 332-2000.
Island and international.

Cambridge $$-$$$
Gregory Town
☎ 335-5080.

Cove Eleuthera $$
Gregory Town
☎ 335-5142
Bahamian and American fare.

Cush's Place $-$$
Gregory Town
☎ 332-5301. Bahamian cooking.

Elvina's $$
Gregory's Town
☎ 335-5032. Bahamian cooking.

Gully's Restaurant and Bakery $$
Bogue
☎ 335-1437
Island fare and baked goods.

Harbour View $$
Rock Sound
☎ 335-0212
Seafood, Bahamian, American.

Hilton's Haven $$
Tarpum Bay
☎ 334-4231.

Ingraham's $$-$$$
Tarpum Bay
☎ 334-4066
Reservations recommended.

Mate and Jenny's Pizza $$
Palmetto Point
☎ 332-2504. Try the conch pizza.

Rainbow Inn $$
Hatchet Bay
☎ 335-0294. Seafood, Bahamian and live entertainment.

Sammy's Place $-$$
Rock Point
☎ 334-2121. Good snacks and salads.

Seven Seas $-$$
North Eleuthera
☎ 333-0011. Seafood and snacks.

Sunset Inn $-$$
Governor's Harbour
☎ 332-2487. Open all day, Bahamian.

THE EXUMA ISLANDS

The islands cover Great Exuma, Little Exuma and the Exuma Cays, a chain that stretches for 90 miles (145km) and includes 365 tiny islands and cays, the majority of which are uninhabited. Altogether the Exuma Islands cover an area of 112sq miles (291sq km). They lie 35 miles (56km) south east of Nassau, and are among the most beautiful, most visited, but least inhabited islands of The Bahamas.

There are scheduled air services and charters from Nassau and Miami to George Town, which is also the official port of entry. Mail boats from Nassau also serve the islands.

The islands have a population of

Unique Village $$
Palmetto Point
☎ 332-1830. Seafood, lamb, steaks and Bahamian cuisine.

Vita's Place $$
Governor's Harbour
☎ 324-2425. Local.

Waldie's $$
Governor's Harbour
☎ 332-2309. Seafood and Bahamian.

Harbour Island

Angela's Starfish Restaurant $$
☎ 333-2253
Excellent Bahamian home cooking.

Arthur's Bakery and Café $
☎ 333-2285
Seafood and fresh baked goods.

Bahama Bayside Café $
☎ 333-2174. Bahamian.

Coral Sands Mediterranean Café $$
☎ 333-2320. Seafood, Bahamian and International.

Devil's Backbone $$
Dunmore Town
☎ 333-2427. Local.

Harbour Lounge $$
On the waterfront
☎ 333-2031.

The Inn $-$$
☎
333-2142
English pub atmosphere and Bahamian and American fare.

Ma Ruby's $$
☎ 333-2161
Seafood and Bahamian specialties.

The Landing $$
☎ 333-2707
Seafood and local specialties.

Pink Sands $
☎ 333-2030.

The Reach and Reachover Restaurant $$
☎ 333-2142. Seafood and Bahamian.

Romora Bay Club $$
☎ 333-2325.

Runaway Hill Club $$
☎ 333-2150. Excellent set dinner menu, reservations required.

Seagrapes $-$$
☎ 333-2439
Snacks, drinks, music and fun.

---

only just over 3500 with about half the population having the surname Rolle, descendants of the slaves owned by the Rolle Family, who owned a 6160 acre (2800 hectare) estate on Great Exuma in the eighteenth century. After Emancipation Lord John Rolle gave the land to the 300 slaves. You can still see the remains of the old slave quarters at Rolleville. Farming and fishing are the main occupations, and the island is noted as a producer of onions. You will also see a lot of breadfruit trees, descendants of plants reputedly bought by a local clergyman from Capt William Bligh of Mutiny on the *Bounty* fame (see Flora and

Fauna in the introduction).

The island was not settled until the late seventeenth century when it was appreciated that salt could be gathered from the shallow lagoons. It became a major producer of salt, although for a time in the eighteenth century, cotton became an important crop until world prices crashed, and you can still see wild cotton growing.

The islands are popular with yachtsmen from around the world because of the sheltered anchorages, and secluded bays and cays. Most of the islanders live on **Great Exuma** and **Little Exuma**, both of which are to the southern end of the chain.

George Town is the main town on Great Exuma, with Williams Town, the main settlement on Little Exuma.

The Exuma International Airport is at Moss Town, just north of George Town, with daily flights from both Nassau and Miami.

National Park

Most of the coastal area is included in the unique **Exuma National Land and Sea Park**, an area administered by The Bahamas National Trust. The 22 mile (35km) long park is the first of its kind in the world, founded in 1958, and is only accessible by boat. It covers the coastal land, the surrounding waters and reefs and the National Trust has the job of protecting everything within its 176sq mile (473sq km) boundaries, especially the prolific wildlife. The park is especially important because it is a refuge for the 'Bahamian dragons', rock iguanas that can grow to 2ft (0.6m) in length. It is also a living aquarium as no surface fishing or trapping is allowed. The islands are rich in wildlife, and you can see hutias, and even wild peacocks, the descendants of a pair of birds abandoned when their owner left for a job in Nassau.

The park attracts both divers and boaters because of the rich undersea life, reefs and caves, and many shipwrecks. **Ocean Rock** is a special feature, a huge underwater valley whose sides are full of caves in which grows a black coral. The feature is known locally as the **Iron Curtain**.

At **Staniel Cay**, you can visit **Thunderball Grotto**, so named because parts of the James Bond film of the same name, was shot here. The grotto has been carved out of a huge rock that juts out of the water. Inside there are stalactites, coral and sponges. Light flickers through cracks in the rock walls casting eerie shadows, and there are a number of entrances some of which can be entered at low tide without submerging. Disney studios used the same location for their mermaid film *Splash*, starring Darryl Hannah and Tom Hanks.

The islands attract yachts from around the world, and many of the people who have winter homes here spend much of their island time sailing. There are a number of small villages on the northern end of Great Exuma such as Moss Town, Steventon and Rolleville perched on the hill above the little quay. You can still see the ruins of the slave quarters from the **Rolle Plantation**.

The fishing here is also excellent, although catches within the park are monitored. The shallow inshore waters provide world-class bone fishing with many trophy fish landed. On the west coast of the island is **Mount Thompson**. Although it is little more than a hillock, it does offer views of The Three Sisters and **Duck Cay** offshore.

George Town is a delightful community that has been serving mariners for centuries, and today yachts cruising the islands stop to take on supplies, or to use the facilities at the full-service marinas. The mail boats dock at Government Wharf where the fishermen also sell their daily catch. There are shops, a bank, post office and a busy, little straw market and delightful homes and cottages. The Government Administration Building is based on Nassau's Government House and contains the commissioner's office, police station, court and jail. Perched on a small rise close to the water is St. Andrew's Anglican Church, built at the beginning of the nineteenth century, with its gleaming white walls and gray roof. 'Shark Lady' Gloria Patience is one of the island's most colorful characters and lives just outside George Town. Even in her seventies, she would regularly take her 13ft (4m) Boston whaler out to catch sharks on a hand-line. The shark's teeth were then used to produce necklaces and other unusual jewelry.

Stocking Island stands about a mile (1.6km) off George Town and there is a ferry for people wanting to spend a day on the beach, shell collecting or exploring the underwater **Mystery Cave**, which is at least 400ft (122m) deep, but no one is quite sure how far it stretches.

There are lots of great dive sites around the islands, such as the shal-

Legacy of slavery

Rolle Town on Great Exuma, is named after John Rolle, who was an American loyalist who after the American Revolution. He accepted a land grant from the English king and moved to the island with his slaves. He was later knighted by the crown, and under the deeds of his land, the estate was handed over to his slaves on the condition that the land never be sold and must be handed down intact from generation to generation. The town is perched on a hill with great views, and the residents take great care over their pretty homes, painted in assorted blues, yellows and pinks.

low **Pagoda Reef** with a wide variety of corals; **Dog and Puppy Reef** with coral towers, pinnacles and

Elizabeth Harbour

trenches and many blue holes in **Elizabeth Harbour.** Experienced divers can also explore the **Stocking Island Cave** close to George Town. It is really a deep water-filled tunnel up to 12ft (4m) high and more than 6ft (2m) wide which extends an unknown length inland.

During April, the islands host the inter-island Family Island Regatta that takes place off George Town. It is one of the few times when the town really does get crowded, but there is a festive atmosphere with parades and partying, bonfires and talent contests.

A small bridge runs between Great Exuma and Little Exuma where **Williams Town** is the largest settlement. The road runs past **Pretty Molly Bay,** so named because a mermaid named Molly is said to appear sometimes at night. You can visit the remains of the **Williams Town Salt Marsh,** where salt used to be collected in shallow pans and gathered after the sun had evaporated the water.

Williams Town is in the far south of the island, a small fishing village and an old settlement. Nearby is **The Hermitage,** formerly a Great House, and now a private home. The ruins of the former slave quarters can still be seen.

INAGUA ISLANDS

Inagua Islands, consisting of Great and Little Inagua, are the most southerly of The Bahamas' islands, and cover 645sq miles (1678sq km). The chain is only 60 miles (97km) from Cuba across the Old Bahama Channel. It is best known for the 290sq mile (754sq km) Bahamas National Trust Park centered on Lake Windsor, which is the sanctuary for 50,000 West Indian flamingos. The sight of thousands of pink flamingos flying against the backdrop of the setting sun is stunning. Although the island's name is an anagram of iguana, none of these reptiles are to be found here. You can see, however, flamingos and many other species of birds, as well as wild donkeys and you might glimpse a wild boar although these animals generally keep to the densest parts of the forest.

The beaches are a nesting ground for the green turtle, and the islands are also the habitat for the rare Inagua freshwater turtle. The islands have a human population of 985, most of whom live in **Matthew Town,** the main settlement. South of Matthew Town is **Southwest Point** with its lighthouse.

The main industry is the production of salt, and Morton Salt produces almost a million pounds every year, using the world's largest solar evaporator.

LONG ISLAND

Long Island, with its cliffs, hills and limestone caves, is believed to have been the third island in The Bahamas visited by Columbus, and a monument commemorates the landing. It is fast becoming popular as a diving area. It is also popular with fishermen, and yachtsmen and hosts a hugely popular annual regatta. It is about 60 miles (97km) from north to south, about one and a half miles wide (3km) and covers 173sq miles (450sq km), and has a population of about 2950. The Tropic of Cancer runs through the island. The Lucayan name for the island was Yuma and Columbus renamed it Fernandina, after the Spanish king.

One of the most striking differences as you travel around the island is between the north and south coasts. There are airports at Stella Maris and Deadman's Cay that have both scheduled and charter flights. Mail boats from Nassau also serve the islands.

Stella Maris in the north is the main resort area with an airport and waterfront where the weekly mail boat docks. Nearby are the remains of the **Adderley's Plantation**, established by Loyalists in the nineteenth century. Cotton was planted but it proved to be an uneconomic crop and the plantation, and others on the island such as Dunmore and Gray, failed. The remains of all three can be seen. Stella Maris is noted for is resort and the offshore Shark Reef where diving instructors hand feed several species of these fish.

South of Stella Maris is the pretty village of **Simms**, one of the oldest settlements on the island, with pastel painted cottages. Many of the houses have charms and mascots to ward off evil spirits. The mail boat calls at Simms once a week to unload cargo and take on board locally grown fruit and vegetables for the market in Nassau. **Salt Pond** is further south and every year is host to the very popular Long Island Regatta.

Clarence Town is the most southerly settlement and the best known because of its two churches – St

Ancient art

Deadman's Cay in the southern half of the island has the largest population, shops, churches, schools, and the commercial airport. The settlement is noted for **Deadman's Cay Cave**, which has some Lucaya paintings on one wall, and many stalactites and stalagmites. The cave leads to the sea and, like those at Simms and Millerton, may have been used by pirates. **Hartford Cave** on neighboring Rum Cay has the best Arawak petroglyphs (stone carvings) in The Bahamas.

Paul's Anglican Church and St. Peter's Catholic Church, both built by Father Jerome. He built St Paul's first, while still an Anglican, and then built St Peter's after he converted to Catholicism. He built both in the style of early New World Spanish missions.

There are scores of dive sites around the island, such as the **Long Island Blue Hole** where you can often see bottlenose dolphins and turtles. The **Ships' Graveyard** is about half a mile (0.8km) off **Cape Santa Maria Beach**, the northern tip of the island, and the 110ft (34m) freighter *Comerbach*, sits on the ocean floor in 100ft (30m) of water. There is spectacular wall diving around **Conception Island** with exceptional visibility. The vertical walls begin in shallow water around 50ft (15m). Other dive sites include Angelfish Reef, Grouper Village, Shark Reef, Flamingo Tongue and Blue Tang Reef.

MAYAGUANA

Mayaguana is an island getaway for those who can get there by boat. There are few tourist facilities and no docks, so tenders are needed to get ashore. The island covers 110sq miles (286sq km) and most of the 312 islanders live in the main village of Abraham's Bay on the south coast.

RUM CAY

This small island 10 miles (16km) by 4 miles (6km) is 35 miles (56km) from San Salvador, and is believed to have been Columbus' second landfall in 1492. He named it Santa Maria de la Conception, but it became the refuge of pirates who felt safe because few vessels were prepared to attack through the treacherous reefs surrounding the island. Port Nelson is on the south coast and the only settlement. For many years the island earned its living producing salt that was shipped to New England where the fishermen used it to preserve their catches. The island got its name after a ship carrying rum foundered on the reefs, and today that ship is one of the many wrecks that attract divers. Another major wreck site is *HMS Conqueror* which sank in 1861 and lies in only 25ft (8m) of water. There is an airstrip and the mail boat calls weekly.

SAN SALVADOR

San Salvador is the island where Columbus first stepped ashore in Fernandez Bay on the morning of 12 October 1492. He wrote: 'even the singing of the birds is such that a man could never wish to leave this place'. The Lucayans originally named the island Guanahani. Long after Columbus changed the name to San Salvador, it was invaded by a British pirate, Captain George Watling, who named it after himself and it was not changed back to San Salvador until 1926.

It is 12 miles (19 km) long, five miles (8km) wide, and covers 63sq miles (164sq km) and has a population of 465. The island is the exposed peak of a submerged mountain that plunges more than 15,000ft (4573m) to the ocean floor. Reefs, caves, drop-offs and 15 miles (24km) of walls attract divers, and the surrounding shallows and flats draw fishermen for the world record sport and bill fishing. There are miles of deserted, sandy beaches, and the island is home to the San Salvador rock iguana.

There are scheduled flights from Nassau and charter flights from Florida to **Cockburn Town**, which is also the official port of entry, where the weekly mail boats from Nassau also dock. The settlement has two small churches with interesting cemeteries, shops, library, police station and court, telephone office and commissioner's offices.

There are several monuments to the Columbus landing, including a cross in **Fernandez Bay**, not far south of Cockburn Town, at the point where scholars think it is most likely he landed. There is also an underwater monument, marking the spot where Columbus' flag ship, the *Santa Maria* is believed to have anchored. A third monument has

nothing to do with Columbus, but commemorates the arrival of the Olympic flame in 1968 on its way from Mount Olympus to Mexico, the host nation.

Memories of Columbus

North of Cockburn Town is **Riding Rock Point** which is recorded in Columbus' log, and the waters offshore are a popular dive site. Further north still, on the north-eastern corner of the island, is **Graham's Harbour**, which is also described by Columbus in his log. He was so impressed by the size of the natural quay, that he wrote it was large enough 'to hold all the ships in Christendom.'

Near the waterfront is The Bahamas Field Station that conducts scientific research and attracts biologists and geologists from around the world (☎ 331-2520). Just to the south is the 160ft (49m) high **Dixon Hill Lighthouse**, built in the mid-nineteenth century. It is kerosene fuelled and is still hand operated.

There is a keeper on duty round the clock, and you can normally get permission to climb the stairs to the observation deck that offers stunning views both out to sea and across the island.

The small **New World Museum** on the east coast near **North Victoria Hill**, has many interesting artifacts from pre-Columbian times when the Lucayans lived on the island, and traces of their settlements have been found. There is another monument to Columbus on **Crab Cay**, which can only be reached on foot. The Chicago Herald erected it in 1892 on the site they believed Columbus landed!

The coast road south then passes **Green Bay** and **Snow Bay**. There are a number of small villages along this stretch of coast but all the land used to be taken up with plantations, and occasional ruins can still be seen.

The road continues past **Pigeon Creek** to the south of the island and **Watling's Castle**. The overgrown ruins are close to the most southerly point on the island, and some people claim it was the pirate's home. It was in fact, the plantation house built in the late eighteenth century by an American Loyalist. The interior of the island consists of a number of large lakes, such as **Great Lake** and **Granny's Lake** and wetlands that are home to a wealth of wild birds.

EATING OUT AND NIGHTLIFE

Exuma Island

Beach Inn $$
George Town
☎ 336-2250. Local.

Castaways $$
Moss Town
☎ 345-0088. Local and international.

Chat and Chill $$
Stocking Island
☎ 358-5010. Local.

Club Peace and Plenty $$-$$$
☎ 336-2551
Elegant, international dining.

Eddie's Edgewater $$
☎ 336-2050. Seafood and Bahamian.

Fisherman's $$
Barraterre, Exuma
☎ 355-5016. Seafood and Bahamian.

Hotel Higgins Landing $$
Stocking Island
☎ 336-2460.

Iva Bowe's Restaurant and Bar $$
Ramsey, Exuma
☎ 345-7014. Seafood and Bahamian.

Kermit's Airport Lounge $-$$
George Town ☎ 345-0002.

La Shante $$
☎ 345-4136
Seafood, fritters, Bahamian fast food.

New Hilltop Sports Bar $$
George Town
☎ 336-2288. International.

Peace and Plenty Beach Inn $-$$
☎ 336-2250. International, Chinese and Bahamian.

Ruth's Deli $-$$
George Town
☎ 336-2596. Light Bahamian fare.

Sam's Place $$
George Town
☎ 336-2579. Seafood, Bahamian.

Silver Dollar $$
George Town
☎ 336-2939. Bahamian cooking.

Places to Visit

The Out Islands

There are few formal attractions in the Out Islands which are mainly visited for their beaches, diving and fishing.

ABACO ISLANDS

Open: from 9.30am to 4pm, Monday and Tuesday, Thursday to Saturday. ☎ 365-4094.

Wyannie Malone Museum

If the museum is not open, ask around because one of the volunteers, who staff it, may well open it up for you. Admission is free but donations are appreciated. ☎ 366-0086.

ANDROS ISLANDS

The small South Andros Museum is in Long Bay. ☎ 369-1688.

Exuma Island, Inagua Island, Long Island & San Salvador

Staniel Cay Yacht Club $$-$$$
☎ 355-2024. Seafood, International.

Towne Café $-$$
George Town
☎ 336-2194. Breakfast and lunch.

Two Turtles Inn $$
George Town
☎ 336-2545. Even the locals know a good thing and come to enjoy the weekly barbecue.

Nightlife

Club La Shante, ☎ 345-1436

Club Peace and Plenty ☎ 336-2551

Eddie's Edgewater Club, ☎ 336-2050

Kermit's, George Town, ☎ 345-0002

Silver Dollar, ☎ 336-2615

Two Turtles ☎ 336-2545

Three Sisters ☎ 358-4040

Dames ☎ 345-0088.

Inagua Island

Cozy Corner $$
☎ 339-1440. Good seafood.

Topps Restaurant and Bar $$
☎ 339-1465. Good seafood.

Long Island

Archer's Pepper Pot $-$$
Deadman's Cay
☎ 338-2005. Bahamian and seafood.

Cape Santa Maria Beach Resort $-$$
☎ 357-1006. Seafood and Bahamian.

Stella Maris Resort Club $$
Bahamian, American and Continental.
☎ 338-2051

San Salvador

Club Mediterranee Caribe $$
☎ 323-8430. Seafood, Bahamian and international.

Riding Rock Inn $$
☎ 331-2631
Seafood and Bahamian.

Accommodation
& Sports facilities

3

ACCOMMODATION

The Bahamas has a wide range of accommodation to suit all tastes and pockets, from top class hotels to delightful guesthouses, self-catering apartments, luxury villas and beach cottages. If you want to eat out and explore quite a lot, it pays to stay in a hotel offering board only. If you want to laze on the beach and not stray far from the hotel, choose a hotel package offering meals as well.

There are also apartments, holiday villas and beach cottages available for short and long rent offering you the privacy of your own accommodation and the flexibility to eat in or out, with cooks and maid service available if required.

Some terms: MAP stands for Modified American Plan i.e. breakfast and dinner included. EP or European Plan means bed only and no meals, and AP for American Plan, means room and all meals. Prices quoted by hotels are for rooms, whether one or two people are sharing, and you may find it difficult to get a reduction if you are traveling alone, but have a go. $ denotes inexpensive accommodation, $$ moderate, and $$$ deluxe.

Note: Many hotels add a series of charges to your hotel bill that can come as a shock if you are not prepared for it. Apart from the Government tax, there is often an additional amount to cover tips to maids, bellboys and other staff, on top of a 15% service charge that may have been added on restaurant and bar bills.

AN A-Z OF ACCOMMODATION

GRAND BAHAMA ISLAND

$$ Bahama Reef Resort and Club

A three story apartment-style complex overlooking an inland waterway, which offers 11 spacious one-bedroom apartments and a three bedroom penthouse suite, all with full kitchens. It has a marina with boats for rent, pool and hot tub.
☎ 373-5580.

$$$ Bahamia

Set in 1000 acres (400 hectares) of lush, tropical gardens with 965 deluxe rooms and suites in the Towers (400) and the adjoining Country Club (565). 9 restaurants from a casual poolside bar and grill to elegant, gourmet dining. Several other bars, lounges and a lively disco. A huge choice of recreational activities from 2 championship golf courses, floodlit tennis and 2 spectacular pools with waterfalls, to fitness area and jogging trail. The Bahamia Casino is one of the most impressive in the Caribbean, featuring a Las-Vegas style revue.
☎ 1-800-545-1300 or 352-9661.

$$$ Bell Channel Inn and Marina

West End
32 luxury 2 and 3 bedroom properties with private beach, pool, clubhouse, tennis and 25 slip marina
☎ 373-1053.

$$ Castaways Resort

Conveniently situated next to a wide range of shops and sporting opportunities in the heart of Freeport. It has recently undergone an upgrade of all its 130 rooms, and is noted for its Yellow Bird Show Room and Flamingo Restaurant. It has pool, sun deck and free beach transportation.
☎ 352-6682.

$$$ Chillingsworth Court Resort

Overlooks the Ruby golf course and offers 15 luxury condominiums set in tropical gardens with pool. Each unit has modern kitchen and private terrace or patio, and the resort offers complimentary scheduled transport
☎ 352-7632.

$$-$$$ Clarion Atlantik Beach and Lucaya Golf and Country Club

175 beachside rooms with 2 restaurants, snack bar, bars, Olympic-size pool, jacuzzi, tennis, golf, shopping arcade, watersports and windsurfing school.
☎ 373-1444.

$$-$$$ Club Viva Fortuna

A new 276-room all-inclusive beachfront resort on the mid-south coast at Churchill Beach with a huge range of activities and watersports, as well as a health and fitness area with an Italian accent.
☎ 373-4000

$$ Coral Beach Hotel and Condos

A small 10-room beachside hotel and condominium block, close to shops, dining, casino and entertainment.
☎ 373-2468.

$$ Deep Water Cay Club

A world class bone fishing resort on the eastern tip of the island, close to 200sq miles (520sq km) of flats and creeks. Accommodation is in 11 comfortable cottages and deluxe cabins. The Club has its own airstrip, custom-designed boats, and outstanding restaurant.
☎ 353-3073.

$$-$$$ Fortune Hills Golf and Country Club

East Sunrise Highway
One, two and three bedroom apartments with restaurant, bar, pool, golf and pro shop.
☎ 373-4500/2222.

$$ Freeport Resort and Club

Rum Cay Drive, West End
49 apartments.
☎ 352-5371.

$$$ Lakeview Manor Club

Offers luxury, designer-decorated studios and one-bedroom apartments with private patio and gourmet kitchen, overlooking the PGA championship Ruby Golf Course. The club offers pool, tennis, patio and barbecue area and free transport to the beach, shops, restaurants and casino.
☎ 352-9789.

$$$ Our Lucaya Golf Resort

Has recently undergone an extensive multi-million dollar refurbishment and has something for everyone. It is situated along a 2-mile (3km) stretch of white sand beach on the south shore with 1350 rooms in three linked resorts close to the Port Lucaya Marketplace. The resorts are Reef Village, Breakers Cay and Lighthouse Pointe. There is a choice of dining from the poolside barbecue to fine, continental cuisine. Entertainment includes the Flamingo Showcase Theatre revue. On-site dive shop, Village Market Promenade, spa & fitness area and tennis. The resort boasts two golf courses: Our Lucaya designed by Dick Wilson, and Our Lucaya Reef, designed by Robert Trent Jones Jr plus the Butch

Harmon School of Golf.
☎ 373-1333.

The 30,000sq ft Casino, the only beachside one on the island, has the full range of gambling plus more than 500 slot machines.
☎ 373-7777.

$$ New Victoria Inn

Offers forty good value rooms, with pool, jacuzzi and free transport to the beach, shops and casino.
☎ 373-3040.

$$$ Ocean Reef Yacht Club and Resort

Bahama Reef Boulevard
An elegant resort with 65 one, two and three bedroom villas, with pool, gym, spa, tennis, golf and fully equipped 54-slip marina.
☎ 373-4662.

$$ Port Lucaya Resort and Yacht Club

Bell Channel Bay Road
With a 100-slip marina, 160 water-front rooms, restaurant, large pool, jacuzzi
☎ 373-9090.

$$ Redwood Motel

Bell Channel Road, West End
24 rooms
☎ 351-7881.

$$-$$$ Royal Islander

The Mall, Freeport
100 rooms
☎ 351-6000.

$$ Royal Palms

Port Lucaya Marina Village
48 rooms with restaurant, bar and pool
☎ 373-9550.

$$ Running Mon Marina and Resort

Kelly Court and Knott's Boulevard, Freeport/Lucaya.

Offers 32 spacious rooms and the Admiral Suite overlooking the full-service 70-slip marina. It has restaurant and lounge, dive shop, and offers deep sea fishing charters and party cruises. There is a complimentary shuttle to the beach, shops and casinos and even a wedding chapel if you want to tie the knot.
☎ 352-6834.

$$-$$$ Xanadu Beach Resort and Marina

Offers 179 luxury rooms and villas along a secluded one mile (1.6km) stretch of beach. It has a choice of restaurants in addition to the popular nightly buffet, bars and entertainment. There is a new vendor's market on the resort's beach. Activities include Beach Olympics, deep-sea fishing, water-sports, sauna, pool, tennis and nearby golf. There is a fully equipped dive area and 77-slip marina.
☎ 352-6782

NEW PROVIDENCE ISLAND

$$ Arawak Inn

West Bay Street
6 rooms
☎ 322-2638.

$$ Aliceanna's Guest House

Hay Street
5 rooms
☎ 352-4974.

$$ Astoria Hotel

West Bay and Nassau Streets
70 ocean-view rooms
☎ 322-8666.

$$ -$$$ British Colonial Hilton

One of Nassau's most famous landmarks, in the heart of downtown, with 240 en-suite rooms and suites, restaurant, bar, pool, beach, health club, sailing, watersports, introductory scuba lessons and deep sea fishing.
☎ 322-3301.

$$$ Breezes

Luxury all-inclusive SuperClubs flagship resort with its own 900ft (300m) beach on Cable Beach, and with 391 spacious rooms and suites. Facilities include all-inclusive meals in a choice of restaurants, snacks, unlimited drinks, as well as entertainment in the Hurricanes disco, Piano Bar and Karaoke Room, and airport transfers. Sports include windsurfing, sailing, kayaking, watersports, fitness area, aerobic classes, floodlit tennis, volleyball, basketball, shuffleboard and putting golf.
☎ 327-6153.

$$ Buena Vista Hotel

In a comfortable old nineteenth-century Colonial mansion with 5 rooms and fine dining, set in 3 acres (1 hectare) of tropical gardens.
☎ 322-2811

$$ Casuarinas of Cable Beach

A really friendly, comfortable and good value 78-room, 4-suite family run hotel with two good restaurants, private beach, bars, lounge, tennis, games room, jet ski, gift shop.
☎ 327-7921

$$$ Clarion Resort South Ocean

238 rooms, with 4 restaurants, bars, championship 72-par golf course designed by Joe Lee, floodlit tennis, watersports, dive center and conference facilities.
☎ 362-4391.

$$ Colony Club Resort

St. Alban's Drive
94 units in tropical gardens with maid service.
☎ 325-4824.

$$ Compass Point Beach Club

20 rooms
☎ 327-4500/800 OUT POST

$$ Coral Harbour Beach House and Villas

8 beachside units and restaurant
☎ 362-2210.

$$ Corner House Hotel

Carmichael Road and Faith Avenue
11 rooms, maid service, restaurant and bar
☎ 361-7445.

$$ Curry's Guest House

Quarry Mission Road
5 rooms
☎ 326-7037.

$-$$ Curry's Motel

Boyd Road
4 rooms
☎ 323-4020.

$$ DeCameron's Inn

Eneas Street
5 rooms
☎ 323-5219.

$-$$ Dillet's Guest House

Strachan Street and Dunmore Avenue.
    7 rooms, bed and breakfast in a traditional Bahamian home
☎ 325-1133.

Above & below: Lucaya Beach Resort, Grand Bahama

$$ Diplomat Inn

Delancy Street
7 rooms close to the beach and downtown
☎ 325-2688.

$-$$ El Greco Inn

West Bay and Augustus Streets
26 comfortable rooms round a central courtyard. Close to beach and all amenities.
☎ 325-1121.

$$ Glowell Motel-Villas Resort

St. Albans Drive
9 units
☎ 356-4943.

$$ Grand Central Hotel

Charlotte Street
34 rooms
☎ 322-8356.

$$$ Graycliff Hotel

West Hill Street
A small luxurious 14-room, 6-suite resort set around a 250-year-old building with wonderful award-winning restaurant set in tropical gardens with pool .
☎ 322-2796.

$$-$$$ Guanahani Village

Cable Beach
35 town houses and 105 oceanfront rooms with pool, tennis and nearby golf
☎ 327-5236.

$$ Harbour Moon Hotel

Bay Street
30 rooms
☎ 328-8120.

$$-$$$ Holiday Inn

Junkanoo Beach
Luxury hotel close to the beach with 115 rooms and 15 suites, restaurant, bar and pool
☎ 1-800-HOLIDAY.

$$ Makeba Beach Hotel

Holiday Drive, South Beach
8 rooms, restaurant, lounge, disco, jerk pit and traditional fare.
☎ 356-2691.

$$ Mignon Guest House

Market Street
6 rooms
☎ 322-4771.

$$ Mondigo Inn

Alexander Boulevard
Nassau Village
8 rooms
☎ 393-0333.

$$ Montagu Beach Inn Hotel

East Shirley Street and Village Road
Small and informal 33-room property with restaurant, lounge, pool and close to the beach
☎ 393-0475.

$ Morris Guest House

Davis Street, Oakes Field
7 rooms
☎ 325-0195.

$$$ Nassau Beach Hotel

Cable Beach
Beautiful Colonial-style hotel with 396 rooms, 7 suites, 6 restaurants, bars, nightclub, pools, tennis and watersports, adjacent to casino and golf .
☎ 327-7711.

$$ Nassau Harbour Club Hotel and Marina

50 comfortable rooms with balconies overlooking the waterfront or pool, and two restaurants, Ivory Coast and Shooters nightclub, catering almost round the clock to visiting yachts folk.
☎ 393-0771.

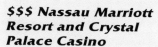

$$$ Nassau Marriott Resort and Crystal Palace Casino

Cable Beach
867 rooms with restaurants and dinner theatre, bars, pool and swimming lagoon, beach, entertainment including the Rainforest Theatre, tennis, squash, racquetball, championship golf course, watersports, and glittering 35,000sq ft casino.
☎ 327-6200.

$$ Ocean Spray Hotel

West Bay Street
29 rooms
☎ 322-8032.

$$ Olive's Guest House

Blue Hill Road
7 rooms
☎ 356-0268.

$-$$ Orange Hill Beach Inn

West Bay Street
Good value, comfortable 32-room inn popular for weddings and honeymoons because of its relative seclusion. It has dining room, pool and shopping trips.
☎ 327-7157.

$$ Orchard Hotel

Village Road
21 rooms set in 2 acres (1 hectare) of gardens with pool and close to the beach
☎ 393-1297.

$$ Park Manor Guest House

Market Street North
33 apartments and rooms with maid service and pool
☎ 325-3554.

$$$ Radisson Cable Beach Casino and Golf Resort

700 rooms set in 7 acres (2.8 hectares) of tropical ocean-side gardens, with 6 specialty restaurants, bars, nightly entertainment, pools, watersports, floodlit tennis, squash, championship golf course, children's camp, activities, Las Vegas style show, conference facilities and the largest casino in the Caribbean.
☎ 327-6000.

$$ Red carpet Inn

Family run inn with 40 rooms, restaurant, bar, pool and entertainment
☎ 393-7981.

$$$ Sandals Royal Bahamian Hotel

A former private home that grew into a luxury all-inclusive property attracting the rich and famous. Facilities include 405 luxury rooms and villas, with 8 restaurants, 7 bars, pools, entertainment, tennis, ballroom, billiard room, health spa, beauty salon, watersports and high tea.
☎ 327-6400.

$$ Sandy Port Beaches Resort

West Bay Street
72 suites, 2 restaurants, pools, tennis
☎ 327-4279.

$$ Sir Charles Hotel

East Street South and Malcolm Road
20 rooms
☎ 322-5641.

$$ Smith's Motel

East Street South
with 20 rooms
☎ 323-6873.

$$ Sun Fun Resorts

Cable Beach
6 suites and 41rooms, Pisces
Restaurant and Lounge, pool
☎ 327-8827.

$-$$ Towne Hotel

George Street
Comfortable, friendly and good value
46-room property, with restaurant,
bar, pool and close to all downtown
amenities.
☎ 322-8450.

$$ West Bay Inn

West Bay Street
40 rooms
☎ 323-1000.

$$-$$$ West Wind Club

West Bay Street
An intimate 54-villa beach property
with snack bar and grill, tennis,
snorkeling, sunfish, rubber rafts and
close to restaurants and amenities.
☎ 327-7211.

PARADISE ISLAND

$$$ Atlantis Paradise Island

A vast, luxury complex consisting of
Beach Towers and Coral Towers with
2300 rooms and suites in beautiful
and imaginative tropical gardens,
with gourmet restaurants, bars,
pool, casino, cabaret show, pool,
watersports and shopping arcades.
Beach Tower ☎ 363-2431 and Coral
Tower ☎ 363-3000.

$-$$ Bay View Village

Bay View Drive
Condominium resort with 30 suites.
Facilities include snack bar, bar,
pools, tennis and shop.
☎ 363-2555.

$$ Chaplin House

Western End
4 rooms
☎363-2918.

$$$ Club Land 'Or

Paradise Beach Road
72 fully equipped one bedroom villas
with kitchens, restaurant.
☎ 363-2400.

$$$ Club Mediterranee

All inclusive 314-room resort set in
21 acres (8.5 hectares) of lovely
grounds with three restaurants, bars,
massive pool, floodlit tennis, tennis
clinics, golf driving range and
chipping green, watersports, daily
activities and nightly entertainment.
☎ 323-8430.

$$-$$$ Comfort Suites

Paradise Island Drive
150 suites with restaurant, bar and
use of Atlantis Paradise amenities
☎ 363-3680.

$-$$ Holiday Inn

Sunspree
Good value high rise hotel with 250
rooms, 2 restaurants, bars, pool,
tennis, spa, aerobic classes, free
bikes, nightclub and comedy club.
☎ 363-2561.

$$$ Ocean Club Golf and Tennis Resort

Paradise Island Drive
59 rooms, suites and villas with
private patio and jacuzzi, set in
lovely tropical grounds, with
restaurants, bars, pool, tennis.
☎ 363-3000.

$$-$$$ Paradise Island Harbour Club and Marina

Paradise Island Drive
16 suites and 23 luxury rooms plus
20-slip marina and free water taxi to
downtown. ☎ 363-2992.

$$-$$$ Pirate's Cove Holiday Inn

Sunspree Resort
On a private beach with 564 rooms, 3 restaurants, large pool, 2 bars, children's club, tennis, watersports, tour desk, nightly entertainment.
☎ 363-2100.

$$$ Sheraton Grand Resort

Casuarina Drive
Luxury 340-room and suite ocean-side resort with specialty restaurants, bars, pool, beach, tennis, golf, daily activities, watersports, and tours.
☎ 363-2011.

$$-$$$ Sunrise Beach Club and Villas

92 units on the beach with pools.
☎ 363-2234.

$$-$$$ Sunshine Paradise Suites

Causarina Drive
Comfortable, fun hotel with 24 rooms, restaurant, bar, pool, beach and watersports.
☎ 363-3955

$$$ Villas in Paradise

Casuarina Drive
20 luxury villas and apartments, close to the beach and all amenities
☎ 363-2998.

$$-$$$ Yoga Retreat

Western End
100 rooms
☎ 363-2902.

OUT ISLANDS

ABACO

$$ Abaco Inn

Elbow Cay
Small inn in Hope Town with 14 suites and 8 villas overlooking the Abaco Sea and the Atlantic Ocean, with noted restaurant, bar, salt water pool, small cove and 3 beaches, snorkeling, watersports, canoeing, fishing and free bike use. There is a dock that can accommodate up to 10 vessels with 5.5ft (1.7m) draft. Use Marsh Harbour Airport.
☎ 1-800-468-8799 or 366-0113.

$$ Ambassador Inn

Marsh Harbour
6 rooms
☎ 367-2022.

$$$ Boat Harbour Marina

On the beach at Marsh Harbour
Luxury accommodation with 58 rooms and villas, fine dining, and a full service 181-slip marina that can take more than 160 boats. Facilities include two pools, hydrojet pool, beach, swim up bar, floodlit tennis and tennis pro shop, shops, watersports, scuba, snorkeling, fishing, and boat and bike rentals. Use Marsh Harbour airport.
☎ 367-2158 and 1-800-468-4799.

$$ Banyan Beach Club Resort

Treasure Cay
21 luxury beachfront rooms and suites
☎ 365-8111.

$$ Bluff House Club

On a private beach on Green Turtle Cay
3 rooms, 15 suites, and 4 villas. Facilities include restaurant, bar,

pool, gift shop, tennis, boat rentals, scuba, snorkeling and fishing, and full service marina with 40 slips. Use Treasure Cay Airport.
☎ 365-4247.

$$ Club Soleil Resort

Hope Town
Offers six uniquely decorated rooms, fine restaurant noted for its seafood and Champagne brunch. Facilities include pool, fishing, scuba, snorkeling, marina, dockage and boat rentals. Use Marsh Harbour Airport.
☎ 366-0003.

$$ Coco Bay Club

Great Guana Cay
8 rooms
☎ 365-5197.

$$ Coco Bay Cottages

Green Turtle Cay
4 cottages. Use Treasure Cay airport
☎ 365-5464 and 1-800-752-0166.

$-$$ Conch Inn Resort and Marina

A comfortable, newly refurbished 9-room hotel by Marsh Harbour, noted for the Conch Inn Café, which offers local and international cuisine. There is a full service 75-slip marina, dive shop and fishing, and boat, bike, scooter, and car rentals are available, plus sightseeing tours. Use Marsh Harbour Airport.
☎ 367-4000.

$$ Different of Abaco and Great Abaco Bonefish Club

18 suites and offers fishing packages. It is an eco-tourism resort with bird sanctuary and nature trails. Use Marsh Harbour Airport
☎ 366-2150.

$$$ Green Turtle Club and Marina

Green Turtle Cay
One of the Out Islands' leading luxury resorts in an idyllic setting by white sand beaches and overlooking crystal clear warm waters. It has 34 rooms and suites and a 35-slip marina. Noted for casual elegance and fine dining. Facilities include restaurant, bar, pool, gift shop, tennis, games room, boat rental, windsurfing and watersports, dive shop, scuba, snorkeling and fishing. Use Treasure Cay Airport.
☎ 1-800-825-5099 or 365-4271.

$$-$$$ Guana Beach Resort

Guana Cay
On a 7 mile (11km) long, near deserted beach with fabulous pristine reefs offshore; has 8 rooms and 7 villas, shops and a 22-slip marina, and is the ideal place to get away from it, lazing in a hammock slung between the palms, sipping tropical cocktails and watching the sunset. Noted for its fine restaurant, to build up an appetite you can enjoy fishing, windsurfing. sunfish sailing, diving and watersports. Use Marsh Harbour Airport.
☎ 365-5133.

$$ Guana Seaside Village

Guana Cay
New beachfront hotel with 8 rooms and 2 suites, restaurant, pool, private beach and dock, snorkeling and fishing.
☎ 365-5106.

$$ Hope Town Harbour Lodge

20 refurbished rooms with ocean, waterfront or poolside views. It has two restaurants, an internationally acclaimed chef and a memorable Sunday brunch. Other facilities

include two bars, pool, beach, games room, watersports, diving, snorkeling, nature walks and bird watching trips, private small boat dock, boating and deep sea fishing. Use Marsh Harbour Airport.
☎ 1-800-316-7844 or 366-0095.

$-$$ Hope Town Hideaways

On the waterfront in Hope Town
Set in 11 acres (18km) of landscaped gardens. The luxury 2-bedroom, 2-bathroom villas have kitchens and maid service is provided. Facilities include pools, fishing, sightseeing, docks and sport boats. The property is close to restaurants, shops, beaches and fishing grounds. Use Marsh Harbour Airport.
☎ 366-0224.

$-$$ Hope Town Villas

Hope Town
Offers good value accommodation in three delightfully refurbished Loyalist cottages, close to sandy beaches, coral reefs and local restaurants. Use Marsh Harbour Airport.
☎ 366-0030.

$$ Linton's Beach and Harbour Cottages

Green Turtle Cay
Offers three historic and comfortable cottages on Long Bay beach with stunning sea views, surrounded by 22 acres (35 hectares) and the Black Sound dock which can accommodate boats up to 60ft (20m). New Plymouth is a short walk away. Use Treasure Cay Airport.
☎ 365-4003 and US 615-269-5482.

$$ Lofty Fig Villas

Marsh Harbour
6 spacious air-conditioned villas. Use Marsh Harbour Airport
☎ 367-2681.

$$ New Plymouth Club and Inn

Green Turtle Cay
Beautifully restored nineteenth-century colonial inn in New Plymouth village, set in lovely gardens. There are 9 rooms, a restaurant offering traditional Bahamian dishes, cocktail bar, pool and patio, fishing trips, snorkeling and nearby tennis . Use Treasure Cay Airport.
☎ 365-4161 and US 908-735-4140.

$$ Pelican Beach Villas

Marsh Harbour
6 villas set on a beachfront peninsula and offering accommodation for up to six. There is a private dock with rental boats and snorkeling on the nearby reefs. Use Marsh Harbour Airport.
☎ 367-3600 and 1-800-642-7268.

$$ Regattas of Abaco

Marsh Harbour
64 rooms
☎ 1-800-322-7757.

$$ Schooner's Landing Resort

Man-O-War-Cay
4 two-bedroom cottages along a lovely beach, with nearby shops and restaurants. Facilities include snorkeling, fishing and sailing. Use Marsh Harbour Airport.
☎ 365-6072.

$$ Sea Spray Resort Villas and Marina

Hope Town
9 one- and two-bedroom ocean or harbor side villas set in 6 acres (2.4 hectares) of grounds, with restaurant, club house, full service deep water 60-slip marina, pool, bike and boat rentals. Use Marsh Harbour Airport.
☎ 366-0065.

$$$ Spanish Cay Resort and Marina

Coopers Town
Small luxury inn on the 185 acres (298 hectares) private island with its own 5,000ft (1500 m) runway, and full service 75-slip marina, or you can fly scheduled air service to Treasure Cay Airport, taxi to Cooperstown and be picked up by the inn's water ferry. There are 5 garden suites and 7 apartments, and facilities include two waterfront restaurants, tennis, five beaches, boats for fishing and diving, privacy and exclusivity. Golf carts are provided so you can explore the island and its beaches. ☎ 365-0083.

$$-$$$ Treasure Cay Resort Hotel and Marina

1,500 acre beach resort with 98 harbour-side rooms and suites, 7 beachfront luxury villas and full service, 150-slip marina. Facilities include restaurant and bar, 18 hole, 72-par, Dick Wilson-designed golf course, tennis, pools and dive center. ☎ 1-800-327-1584.

$$ Turtle Hill Villas

Hopetown
4 two-bedroom villas overlooking an inviting freshwater swimming pool with private access to a vast, pristine beach. Use Marsh Harbour Airport. ☎ 366-0557.

$$-$$$ Walker's Cay Hotel and Marina

Walker's Cay
Secluded, one resort tropical island with outstanding diving and fishing, and full service, deep water 75-slip marina with port of entry facilities. It has 62 luxury rooms, 4 suites and 4 villas. Facilities include restaurants, bars, boutique, two pools, tennis, lawn games, dive shop, scuba, snorkeling, fishing and beautiful beaches. It has its own paved runway and seaplane ramp. Use Walker's Cay Airport. ☎ 1-800-WALKERS or 352-5252.

ANDROS

$$ Andros Island Bonefishing Club

Cargill Creek
12 rooms
☎ 368-5167.

$$-$$$ Andros Lighthouse Yacht Club Marina

Andros Town
Offers full lodging with 12 luxury rooms and 8 suites, gourmet restaurant, cocktail lounge, pool, tennis, scuba, snorkeling and 20-slip marina. Use Andros Town Airport. ☎ 368-2305.

$$ Chickcharnie's Hotel

Fresh Creek
13 rooms
☎ 368-2492.

$$ Conch Sound Resort Inn

Conch Sound
12 rooms
☎ 329-2060.

$$ Emerald Palms By The Sea

Driggs Hill, South Andros
Located right on the beach with 19 rooms, good restaurant, great fishing and snorkeling, and close to one of the largest reefs in the western hemisphere. Facilities include dining room, pool, tennis, day sailing, sunfish, speedboats, fishing, diving, scooters, car rental, sightseeing tours and windsurfing. Use Congo Town Airport. ☎ 369-2661.

$$ Glatos Bonefishing Club

Johnson Bay
14 rooms
☎ 369-4669.

$$ Landmark Hotel

Fresh Creek
20 rooms
☎ 368-2082.

$$ Mangrove Cay Inn

Mangrove Cay
6 rooms and 2 suites, with restaurant, gift shop, fishing, shelling and unspoiled beaches. Use Mangrove Cay Airport.
☎ 369-0069.

$$ Point of View

Fresh Creek
28 rooms
☎ 327-3430.

$$-$$$ Small Hope Bay Lodge

Fresh Creek, Andros
Very friendly all-inclusive establishment popular with divers, which has been under the same family management for more than 35 years. There are 17 cottages on the beach, good restaurant and very relaxed atmosphere. Facilities include dining room, bar, games room, hot tub, snorkeling, dive boats, diving, fishing, windsurfers, sailboats, cycles, boutique and flight pick ups. Use Andros Town Airport.
☎ 368-2013/4 and 1-800-223-6961.

$$ Sunrise Inn By The Sea

Kemps Bay
12 rooms
☎ 369-1640.

Caption

$$ White Sands Beach Hotel

Mangrove Cay
20 rooms
☎ 369-0159.

BERRY ISLANDS

$$ Chub Cay Club

Chub Cay
41 rooms
☎ 325-1490.

$$-$$$ Great Harbour Cay Club

Great Harbour Cay
Offers 18 luxury villas on the beach and 2 townhouses by the full service 85-slip marina. There are three restaurants and facilities include bars, yacht club, pool, airstrip, store, meeting facilities, yacht charters, bicycles, boat rental, limited golf and tennis, fishing, snorkeling and diving. Use Great Harbour Cay Airport.
☎ 367-8838, 1-800-343-7256 or US 941 921-9084.

$$ Little Whale Cay Hotel

Little Whale Cay
12 rooms
☎ 326-9216.

BIMINI

$$ All My Children Hotel

Alice Town
33 rooms
☎ 347-3334.

$$ Bimini Bay Guest House

Alice Town
18 rooms
☎ 347-2171.

$$ Bimini Beach Club and Marina

Alice Town
40 rooms
☎ 359-8228.

$$$ Bimini Big Game Fishing Club, Hotel and Marina

Alice Town, North Bimini
Features an 80-slip marina, and 44 room/suites and 12 cottages, with two restaurants, three bars, pool, store and gift shop, tennis, scuba and boat rentals. Use North Bimini or South Bimini Airport.
☎ 347-3391 and 1-800-737-1007.

$$ Bimini Blue Water

Alice Town, North Bimini
Small comfortable and friendly inn with 7 rooms and suites and 2 cottages, catering specially for the sports angler. The Anchorage Dining Room and Bar specializes in island and Bahamian dishes. Facilities include restaurant, bar, pool, scuba, snorkeling, yacht charters and full service 36-slip marina. Use North Bimini or South Bimini Airports.
☎ 347-3166.

$-$$ Compleat Angler

Alice Town
12 rooms in the most popular and liveliest joint in town, with bar, boating, fishing and diving.
☎ 347-3122.

$$ Sea Crest Hotel and Marina

Alice Town
13 rooms, 18 slips, fishing charters
☎ 347-3071.

$$ South Bimini Yacht Club

Alice Town
15 rooms
☎ 347-4444.

CAT ISLAND

$$ Bridge Inn

New Bight
Comfortable, good value inn with 12
rooms and close to the beach. There
is a restaurant and bar, with car, bike
and boat rental available. Use New
Bight Airport.
☎ 342-3013.

$$-$$$ Fernandez Bay Village

Fernandez Bay
Offers open air dining under the
stars, miles of beautiful beaches and
13 beach-front villas and cottages.
Facilities include restaurant, bar,
store, paddle tennis, sailboats, bikes,
paddle boards. Boston whalers,
lagoon excursions, scuba, snorkeling, water skiing, boat trips,
watersports. Use New Bight Airport.
☎ 342-3043, 1-800-940-1905 and US
(954) 474-4821.

$$ Greenwood Beach Resort

Port Howe
Very comfortable, 20 room resort on
8 miles (13km) of beach ideal for
shore diving. There is a large
oceanfront restaurant and lounge,
beachfront gazebos, pool, full scuba
facilities, snorkeling, shelling,
exploration excursions and fishing
charters. Use New Bight Airport.
☎ 342-3053.

$$ Hawk's Nest Resort and Marina

Hawk's Nest
10 rooms, villa, with restaurant and
lounge, 4,600 foot (1,400 m)
airstrip, 28-slip marina, snorkeling,
diving, fishing and miles of beach.
☎ 357-7257.

$$ Orange Creek Inn

Orange Creek
16 rooms across from the beach
☎ 342-3090.

$$ Pigeon Point Beach Club

Pigeon Cay
7 cottages on a secluded 4-mile
beach plus 7 suites and 8 rooms,
beach bar, canoes and watersports
☎ 354-5084.

$$ Sea Spray Hotel

Orange Creek
14 rooms and a suite; ocean-side
dining; fishing, sightseeing, bike and
car rentals. Use Arthur's Town
Airport.
☎ 354-4116.

CROOKED ISLAND

$$-$$$ Pittstown Point Landings

Pittstown Point
Offers spectacular diving and fishing,
with 12 spacious, comfortable
rooms, restaurant and miles of
beach. There is world-class deep sea
and bone fishing, and scores of dive
sites along the offshore 60-mile
(97km) long wall with several
shipwrecks, many of them rarely
explored. There is also a fascinating
conservation scheme. You can fly in
to Pittstown Point (private planes) or
Colonel Hill Airports.
☎ 344-2507.

Deep Water Cay

$$-$$$ Deep Water Cay Club
On a private island 125 miles
(201km) east of Florida's Palm

Beach, and is famous for its bonefish and permit catches. Custom designed boats and experienced guides ensure the fishing trip of a lifetime. The club has excellent facilities with 7 cottages and 2 houses, good restaurant, and its own 3200-foot (1000m) hardpan private airstrip Use Deep Water Cay or Freeport Airport.
☎ 353-3073 and US 954-359-0488.

ELEUTHERA

$-$$ Cambridge Villas

Gregory Town
13 rooms and 2 apartments, restaurant and bar, with fishing, surfing, snorkeling and scuba diving available. Use North Eleuthera or Governor's Harbour Airport.
☎ 335-5080.

$$-$$$ Cigatoo Resort

Governor's Harbour
22 spacious rooms and suites set in landscaped gardens with bar, pool, tennis, fishing and snorkeling
☎ 332-3060.

$$$ Club Mediterranee

Governor's Harbour
A sprawling all inclusive 288-room resort with restaurants, bars, theatre, disco, ballroom, boutique, pool, tennis, games room, fishing, watersports
☎ 323-8430 (Note: Currently closed)

$$ Cocodimama

Governor's Harbour
Bahamian colonial villa and 3 cottages with 12 rooms
☎ 332-3150.

$$ Cove Eleuthera

Gregory Town
Lies between two coves, and the 26 rooms are in seven tropical buildings

set in the extensive grounds. There is a restaurant, bar and pool and facilities for tennis, bicycle rentals, scuba trips, snorkeling and kayaking from the beach with cars and bikes available to explore the island. Use North Eleuthera or Governor's Harbour Airports. ☎ 1-800-552-5960 or 335-5142.

$ Hilton's Haven

Tarpum Bay
10 attractive rooms, each with their own private patio. The restaurant is noted for its island cuisine although it also offers international dishes. It is a one-minute walk from the beach. Fishing and watersports can be arranged, and rental cars and bikes are available. Use Rock Sound Airport.
☎ 322-7849.

$-$$ Laughing Bird Apartments

Governor's Harbour
4 affordable and comfortable apartments and a house, each with fully equipped kitchenette and private patio or balcony overlooking the beach. Close to the shops and all amenities and sports. Use Governor's Harbour Airport.
☎ 332-2012.

$$ Palmetto Shores Vacation Villas

South Palmetto Point
15 fully equipped villas on the waterfront, close to the shops and restaurants. There are facilities for wind surfing tennis, snorkeling, and deep-sea fishing, and bikes are available. Use Governor's Harbour Airport.
☎ 332-1305.

$$ Rainbow Inn

Hatchet Bay
Small, friendly inn with 4 studio

apartments and two and three bedroom villas, with restaurant and bar overlooking the water, pool, tennis, fishing, and free use of bikes and snorkeling gear. Use Governor's Harbour.
☎ 335-0294 and 1-800-688-0047.

$$ Richard and Carmen's Tuckaway Hotel

Governor's Harbour
10 rooms
☎ 332-2591.

$$ Unique Village

North Palmetto Point
10 spacious rooms, 2 apartments and 2 villas, all with breathtaking views over the miles-long beach. There is a restaurant and bar and free use of snorkeling equipment and nearby tennis. Use Governor's Harbour Airport.
☎ 332-1830.

$$ Venla Club

Rock Sound
144 rooms
☎ 344-4055.

EXUMA

$$ Club Peace and Plenty

George Town
Named after the English ship that brought Lord Denys Rolle to Exuma in 1783 to establish a cotton plantation. It has 35 deluxe rooms and suites with private balconies, and excellent candle-lit restaurant under the control of chef Pierre offering Bahamian and international cuisine. There is a free ferry to their Stocking Island Beach Club, with bar, pool, sunfish, sailboats, tennis, boutique, bikes, fishing, snorkeling, sailboats and windsurfing. Use

Exuma International Airport.
☎ 336-2551 and 1-800-525-2210.

$$$ Coconut Cove

George Town
Intimate accommodation with ten rooms and the Paradise Suite, all on the beach. There is a gourmet restaurant, outside cocktail bar and pool, tropical fish pond, boat rentals, scuba, snorkeling, boating and fishing. Use Exuma International Airport.
☎ 336-2659.

$$ Emerald Bay Marina

Ocean Bight
Due to open mid-2002 and part of a 470-acre resort including Greg Norman championship golf course and 229-room Four Seasons luxury hotel, spa and casino.

$$ Hotel Higgins Landing

Stocking Island
5-cottage resort on the fabulous sandy beaches. Use Exuma International Airport
☎ 336-2460.

$$ Mount Pleasant Suites Hotel

George Town
23 suites set in landscaped gardens with pool
☎ 336-2960.

$$-$$$ Peace and Plenty Beach Inn

George Town
16 deluxe rooms with private balconies, on the waterfront. There is a restaurant, bar, pool and fishing dock, and free shuttle bus to and from Club Peace and Plenty with reciprocal dining available. Facilities also include boat rental, sunfish,

scuba, snorkeling and deep-sea fishing. Use Exuma International Airport.
☎ 336-2250.

$$ The Palms at Three Sisters

Mount Thompson
12 large rooms and 3 villas with kitchenettes, each with private balcony overlooking the beach and sea. There is a waterside restaurant. Use Exuma International Airport.
☎358-4040.

$$ Regatta Point

George Town
6 fully equipped apartments and one efficiency, surrounded by the waters of Elizabeth Harbour. Although it offers its own 'island' privacy, it is only a minute's walk from the town with all its amenities. Facilities include boat rentals, sunfish, bikes, snorkeling, fishing charters, bone fishing, scuba and car rentals. Use Exuma International Airport.
☎ 336-2206.

$$-$$$ Staniel Cay Yacht Club

Staniel Cay
Facilities for divers, yachtsmen and vacationers with 5 delightful cottages and a guesthouse sleeping six. There is excellent diving with gear for rent, and tank filling facilities, and bone reef fishing and guides are available. Other facilities include full service 20-slip marina, free use of Boston whalers, sailboats, gift shop and fishing trips. Use Staniel Cay Airport.
☎ 355-2024 and US 954-467-8920.

$$ Two Turtles Inn

George Town
Small, comfortable and friendly 14 room inn overlooking Elizabeth Harbour, and close to the shops and amenities. There is a restaurant offering open-air dining and native and American dishes, bar, snorkeling, scuba, fishing and boat charters. Bike, moped and jeep rental. Use Exuma International Airport.
☎ 336-2545.

HARBOUR ISLAND

$$-$$$ Coral Sands Hotel

Set on the famous 3 mile (5km) long pink beach and offers 23 luxury rooms, 8 suites and 2 villas set in 14 acres (6 hectares) of grounds which run to the outskirts of historic Dunmore Town. It offers restaurant, bar, games room, floodlit tennis, sailboats, rowboats, snorkeling, surfriders, aqua-view boards, water-skiing, as well as bike, car and motor bike rental. Use North Eleuthera Airport.
☎ 333-2350 and 1-800-468-2799.

$$$ Pink Sands

Set in 16 acres (6 hectares) of tropical gardens with 800ft (244m) of beach, has just undergone extensive refurbishment. It has two restaurants with menus created by award winning chef Peter Birkwiesser. Accommodation is in 20 delightful one- and two-bedroom cottages. Facilities include dining room, bar, lounge, library, tennis, exercise room, boating, diving, watersports and pool. The 16-acre (6.5 hectare) grounds of woodlands and tropical gardens are a designated bird reserve. Use North Eleuthera Airport.
☎ 333-2030 and 1-800-OUTPOST.

$$-$$$ Romora Bay Club

Luxury accommodation on a former private estate fronting the water-front and a short walk along a tropical path to the beach. There are

30 rooms and 4 suites. The restaurant specializes in Bahamian cuisine, and there is a waterfront bar. Facilities include tennis, full service dive shop, full scuba program, snorkeling, windsurfing, sailing, fishing and tennis. Use North Eleuthera Airport.
☎ 333-2325 and 1-800-327-8286.

$$$ Runaway Hill Club

Intimate 10-room inn overlooking the pink sand beach, with gourmet dining room, bar, pool and snorkeling gear. Use North Eleuthera Airport.
☎ 333-2150 and 1-800-728-9803.

$$-$$$ Valentine's Yacht Club and Inn

39 rooms and a popular retreat with divers, watersports enthusiasts and yachtsmen. It has a full service, 39-slip marina, restaurant, tennis, pool and hot tub, fishing and close to the beaches
☎ 333-2141 and 1-800-688-4752.

LONG ISLAND

$$ Cape Santa Maria Beach Resort

12 beachside cottages set in delightful gardens, formerly part pf the Adderley Plantation. There is a good restaurant. Facilities include bar, entertainment, marina, pools, games room, boating, tennis, water-skiing, snorkeling, sailing and fishing. Use Stella Maris Airport.
☎ 338-5273.

$$ Stella Maris Inn

42-room, plantation-style resort with restaurant and bar, a choice of 8 beaches, snorkeling, diving, fishing, 15-slip marina, car and plane rentals. Use Stella Maris Airport
☎ 359-8353.

SAN SALVADOR

$$-$$$ Riding Rock Inn and Marina

Cockburn Town
18 deluxe oceanfront rooms, and 24 others, with restaurant, Driftwood Lounge and pool. Facilities include tennis, scuba, snorkeling, fishing and marina. Use San Salvador Airport.
☎ 331-2631 and 1-800-272-1492.

SPORT FACILITIES

Because of the strong British tradition, cricket, rugby and soccer are all played, as well as golf and tennis. The cricket season lasts from March to November, and matches are played every Saturday and Sunday during the season at the Lucayan Cricket Club on Grand Bahama, and the Haynes Oval, West Bay Street in Nassau. Play usually starts at noon.

For the visitor, there is a huge range of sporting opportunities from swimming and scuba diving, to hiking and tennis, or having a game of cricket with one of the local teams. There is boating, cycling, golf, sailing, squash, water skiing, parasailing, horseback riding and, of course, fishing either from shore or boat. The eastern coast offers stronger swell for windsurfing and surfing but the seas can sometimes be very rough and care is needed, while the west coast beaches offer safe swimming.

Most hotels offer a variety of sports and water activities, and dive operators offer all levels of instruction. You can learn what it is all about and progress to advanced level if you have the time. Walking is great fun and there are lots of trails but have stout, non-slip footwear and a waterproof. Protect yourself against insects, carry adequate drinking water and keep an eye on the time, because night falls quickly and you don't want to be caught out on the trail after dark.

CYCLING

Bikes are a good way of getting around and getting a tan, and can easily be rented on most of the islands.

FITNESS GYMS/ HEALTH CENTERS

Many of the large hotels and resorts offer health and fitness facilities.

FISHING

Fishing is an island pursuit, and many islanders will fish for hours from waterfront walls, from the beach or riverside. There is year-round world-class deep sea and game fishing for Atlantic blue marlin, skipjack, blackfin and yellowfin tuna, also called allison, which can weight over 100lb (45kg), wahoo and white marlin, which can weigh more than 100lb (45kg) and the fighting sailfish. Blue marlin weighing 300 to 500lb (135 to 225kg) are regularly caught although fish weighing more than 1,000lb (450kg) have been caught.

Countless records have been made and broken in The Bahamas for marlin, wahoo, dolphin, swordfish and other big game fish. Snapper, bonefish, permit, pompano, tarpon, grouper, bonito and barracuda can all be caught close to shore. Mako, blue, tiger and hammerhead are among the several species of shark that can be found off the islands. Mako sharks up to 400lb (180kg) have been landed. Around the reefs there is an abundance of grouper, jack crevalle, mutton snapper and yellowtail snapper.

Dorado is usually called dolphin (not the mammal but the fish also called mahi-mahi).

There are many guides and charter boats for hire. Prices vary enor-mously depending on the vessel, number of lines allowed and facilities offered. You can negotiate a half-day's bone fishing for two, with guide, from about $100, while a crewed boat and tackle for deep sea fishing will cost from $400 for a half day, and from $600 for a full day.

GOLF

There are some great golf courses in The Bahamas, many of them championship courses. Three of the courses on Grand Bahama have been on the PGA Tour approved list – the Ruby and Emerald Courses at Bahamia, and the third at the Clarion Resort, all between Freeport and Lucaya.

The 6,824-yard par-72 Country Club course, Bahamia, is the island's oldest, built in 1963 and designed by Dick Wilson. For many years it was the home course of Masters' champion Craig Woods, and the course is designed in such a way that each green and fairway is separated from the next by tropical underbrush and pine trees, so that golfers have a feeling of privacy. ☎ 352-6721.

The 6,750 yard par-72 Ruby course winds its way through lush forest, and the fourth, a 384 yard, par 4 left dogleg, is regarded as the signature hole. It was designed and built by Joe Lee in 1967 – and features 78 bunkers. The 6,679-yard par-72 Emerald course was also built by Dick Wilson and opened in 1965 ☎ 352-6721. The other course is the 6916-yard, 18-hole Fortune Hills Golf and Country Club. It is really a 9-hole course with double tees so that it can be played as 18 holes. ☎ 373-4500.

Our Lucaya Golf Resort boasts two 72-par courses, one designed by the legendary Trent Jones Jr. and the other by Dick Wilson ☎ 373-1066.

SPORTS FACILITIES

Other courses are:
The 7606 yard par-72 Joe Lee designed South Ocean Beach and Golf Resort, New Providence Island, ☎ 362-4391;

the challenging 6,770 yard par-72 Dick Wilson designed Sun International Paradise Island Resort, ☎ 363-3925; the 7040 yard par-72 Nassau Marriott Resort and Crystal Palace Casino course designed by Jim McCormick, Cable Beach, ☎ 327-6000;

the 9 hole 36-par semi private Fortune Hills Golf Course, Freeport ☎ 373-4500;

Treasure Cay Beach Resort and Marina's 18 hole, par-72, Dick Wilson designed course, Abaco Island, ☎ 365-8578; and the exclusive Cotton Bay Club 18 hole, par-72 7,000 yard course designed by Robert Trent-Jones, Eleuthera ☎ 1-800-334-3523.

HORSE RIDING

Grand Bahama
Pinetree Stables, ☎ 373-3600

New Providence
Harbourside Riding Stables, Paradise Island, ☎ 326-3733

Happy Trails, Coral Harbour, ☎ 362-1820

HIKING
There are some spectacular walks around the coast and inland. It is essential to drink plenty of water and take frequent rests, as the walking may be tiring, and wear sensible, sturdy footwear.

SCUBA/DIVING
The waters of The Bahamas offer some of the best diving in the world. The waters are warm and remarkably clear with excellent visibility. Water temperatures range from the low 70s F (low 20s C) in the winter, to the high 80s F (low 30s C) in the summer. Visibility of 150ft to 200feet (46m to 61m) is not uncommon, but reduces considerably after cool nights in the winter.

The reefs are easily accessible and they teem with marine life. You can hand feed sharks, swim with dolphins and mingle with stingrays. Many of the reefs and shipwrecks are close to the shore, while there are walls, drop-offs, caves and tunnels to explore in deeper waters. There are the Bahama Trenches and Banks, and the third largest barrier reef in the world, and shipwrecks galore. The reefs and marine life are so beautiful that they have been used as locations for scores of films including Disney classics and some of the James Bond films. There are literally thousands of excellent dive sites and it is impossible to mention them all, but among the best are:

Abacos Islands:
The Barge, Barracuda Alley, Catacombs, Cathedral, Pelican Cay Land and Sea Park, Green Turtle Cay, Meghan's Mesa, Providence Channel, Queen's 11, Sandy Cay, Shark Rodeo and Shark Canyon, Spiral Canyon, Sue's Reef, Tarpon Wall, Towers, Wayne's World, and wrecks Bonita, San Jacinto and Adirondacks with her cannon in Devil's Hole.

Andros:
Alex and Cara Caverns, Barge Wreck, Black Forest, the Blue Hole, Giant Staircase, Great Barrier Reef, Over the Wall and Tongue of the Ocean.

Berry Islands:
Bond's Cay (named after 007), Chub Cay, Great Harbour Cay, Mama Rhoda Rock,

Bimini:

Bimini Barge, Concrete ship Sapona, Hawksbill Reef, Little Caverns, Off the Wall, Rainbow Reef, Alley, Turtle Rocks, Victory Reef.

Cat Island:

Blue Holes, Columbus Point, First Basin Wall, Tartar Bank, White Hole Reef.

Eleuthera:

Pinnacles, Split Reef, and shipwrecks in Yankee Channel

Exuma:

Angelfish Blue Hole, Crab Cay Blue Hole, Exuma National Land and Sea Park, Iron Curtain, Lobster Reef, Mystery Cave (Stocking Island), Ocean Rock, Pagoda Reef, Stingray Reef and Thunderball Grotto.

Grand Bahama sites provided by UNEXSO:

Shallow dive sites (generally in 15-18ft (4.5-5.5m) of water – Fish Farm, Pillar Castle, Rainbow Reef, Round-about, Sea Hunt and Treasure Reef, so called because in the 1960s almost $500,000 of silver coins was found in the area.

Medium dive sites – Anchors Away, Angels Camp, Ann's Paradise, Arrow Point, Ben's Blue Hole, East Reef Caribe, East Ann's Paradise, Etheridge Creek, Hippie's Wreck, Octopussy Garden, Papa Dock Wreck, Picasso's Gallery, Pretender Wreck, Reef Caribe, Rose Garden, Spid City, Ugly Duckling Wreck and West Ann's Paradise.

Deep Reef sites – Blair Reef 1 and 11, Caves 1 and 11, East Reef, Gale's Grotto, Littlehale's Lair, Lucayan Ridge, Orson Wells, Moray Manor 1, 11 and 111, Plate Reef, Pygmy Caves and Theo's Wreck, a 230 foot-long freighter in 100 feet of water.

Harbour Island:

The Arch, Blow Hole, Current Cut, Civil War Train Wreck, Devil's Backbone, The Plateau.

Long Island:

Angelfish Reef, Grouper Valley and Village, Long Island Blue Hole, Cape Santa Maria Ship's Graveyard, Guana Cay, Shark Reef, Southampton Reef, Conception Island Wall.

New Providence Island:

Disney's 20,000 Leagues Beneath The Sea, Bond films For Yours Eyes Only, Thunderball and Never Say Never, plus hits like Splash, Cocoon and Jaws The Revenge, all had under water shots filmed here. The coast from Delaporte Point to the Southern Banks has reefs galore, walls and leads to the Tongue of the Ocean, and there is excellent diving off Paradise Island. Top dive sites include: Bahama Mama – one of the latest wrecks sunk intentionally in 50 feet (15m) of water to create an artificial reef – Barracuda Shoals, Bond Wrecks, Fish Hotel, Goulding Cay, Lost Ocean Hole, the Mahoney Wreck, Shark Wall and Shark Buoy, Tears of Allah, Tunnel Well,

Rum Cay:

Pinder's Pinnacle, Summer Point Reef and wreck of HMS Conqueror,

San Salvador:

Basket Case, Devil's Claw, Double Caves, Great Cut, Snapshot reef, Telephone Pole and wreck of the Frescate.

Note: If you are a diver, remember to bring your certification and log book with you. Dive operators will not allow you to dive or get air fills without it

Dive operators include:

ABACO ISLANDS

Brendal's Dive Shop,
Green Turtle Club, ☎ 365-4411

Abaco Dive,
Marsh Harbour, ☎ 367-4646

Dive Abaco ☎ 367-2787

Hope Town Dive Shop ☎ 366-0029

Maitlon Lowe ☎ 366-0133

Man-O-War ☎ 366-2222

Sea Below Dive Shop ☎ 352-5252

Spanish Cay Diving and Watersports,
Cooperstown ☎ 365-0083

Walker's Cay Undersea Adventures
☎ 1-800-327-8150/352-5252

Andros

Andros Scuba centre,
Nicholl's Town ☎ 329-2515

Andros Undersea Adventure,
Fresh Creek ☎ 368-2795

Seascape Inn,
Mangrove Cay ☎ 369-0342

Small Hope Bay Lodge,
Fresh Creek, ☎ 368-2014

Berry Islands

Chub Cay Undersea Adventures
☎ 325-1490

Great Harbour Cay ☎1-800-343-7256

Bimini

Bill and Nowdla Keefe's Bimini
Underseas ☎ 347-3089

Scuba Bimini Dive Centre
☎ 1-800-848-4073

Cat Island

Fernandez Bay Village,
☎ 1-800-940-1905 or 342-3043

Cat Island Dive Centre, Hotel
Greenwood Inn, ☎ 342-3053

Crooked Island

Piitstown Point Landings,
☎ 344-2505

Eleuthera

Cove Eleuthera, ☎ 335-5142

Exuma

Exuma Dive Centre, George Town
☎ 336-2390

Exuma Scuba Adventures
☎ 336-2893

Grand Bahama

Caribbean Divers, Bell Channel Inn
☎ 351-6272

Grand Bahama Watersports, Lucaya
☎ 373-6775

Left: Wreck diving

Below: Kayak Nature Tours, Grand Bahama

Opposite page: Charter a seaplane for those more out of the way places

Ocean Safari, Ocean Reef Resort ☎ 373-3217

Sun Odyssey Divers, Silver Palm Court ☎ 373-4014

UNEXSO, Port Lucaya ☎ 373-1244

Xanadu Undersea Adventures, Xanadu Beach Resort ☎ 352-3811

Harbour Island

Manuel's Dive Station Romora Bay Club, ☎ 1-800-327-8286/333-2323

South Eleuthera Divers ☎ 334-4083

Valentine's Dive Centre ☎ 333-2309

Long Island

Stella Maris Resort Club, ☎ 1-800-426-0466 or 338-2050

New Providence Island

Bahama Divers, ☎ 393-6054

Coral Divers ☎ 362-1263

Dive, Dive, Dive, Coral Harbour ☎ 362-1401

Dive Nassau, Bay and Deveaux Streets ☎ 356-5170

Diver's Haven, East Bay Street ☎ 394-8960

Nassau Scuba Centre Coral Harbour ☎ 362-1964

Nassau Undersea Adventures, South Ocean ☎ 362-4171

Stuart Cove's Dive South Ocean ☎ 362-5227

Sun Divers, British Colonial Beach Resort ☎ 325-8927

Sunskiff Divers, Coral Harbour ☎ 362-1979

San Salvador

Riding Rock Inn ☎ 331-2631

Walker's Cay

Walker's Cay Undersea Adventures, Walker's Cay Hotel and Marina, ☎ 1-800-327-8150

Note: There is a recompression chamber at UNEXSO in Port Lucaya.

The following offer shark dives:

Dive, Dive, Dive

Nasau Scuba Centre

Stella Maris Resort

Stuart Cove's Dive South Ocean

UNEXSO

Walker's Cay Undersea Adventures

Xanadu Undersea Adventures

Another fun way to dive and explore the islands is to stay on board a day ship rather than in a hotel. The following live-aboard boats are available:

Blackbeard's Cruises ☎ 1-800-327-9600/US 305-888-1226

Bottom Time Adventures ☎ 1-800-234-8464/US 954-921-7798

MV Ballymena ☎ 1-800-241-4591/394-0951

Nekton Diving Cruises ☎ 1-800-899-6753/US 954-463-9324

Sea Dragon ☎ US 954-533-0161

Sea Fever Diving Cruises ☎ 1-800-443-3837/US 305-531-3483

SQUASH

There are facilities at many resort hotels and in Freeport and Nassau, including The Village Squash Club, Village Road, New Providence ☎ 393-1580.

TENNIS

There are many courts on all the islands and several are floodlit. Most hotels have their own facilities and you can also play on public courts. If newly arrived on the island, book a court early in the morning or late in the afternoon when it is cooler until you get used to the heat.

WATER SPORTS AND AQUATIC ACTIVITIES

Available at all resorts and most large hotels and range from Hobie Cats to jet skis, windsurfers and Sunfish. Experts are also on hand to teach you how to sail, water ski and parasail. Water skiers must operate only in designated areas, and always well away from swimmers.

Note: It is advisable to book water sport activities through your hotel or with accredited operators as some of those offering these facilities on the beaches are not insured in case of accidents.

YACHTING, MARINAS AND BERTHING FACILITIES

Yachts, motorboats and fishing boats are available for charter for day sailing, sightseeing, fishing and diving, and longer trips.

There are marinas at the following:

Abaco

Elbow Cay – Lighthouse Marina, Soleil Resort and Marina

Great Abaco – Abaco Outboard Engines, Boat Harbour Marina, Conch Inn Marina, Harbour View Marina, Marsh Harbour Marina, Mangoes Marina, Sea Spray Marina and Triple J Marina.

Andros

Andros Lighthouse Yacht Club and Marina, Cargill Creek Marina

Berry Islands
Chub Cay Club Marina, Great Harbour Cay Marina,

Bimini
Bimini Beach Club and Marina, Bimini Big Game Fishing Club, Bimini Blue Water, Cat Cay Yacht Club, Sea Crest Hotel and marina, Weech's Dock

Eleuthera
Cape Eleuthera Marina, Cotton Bay Club, Davis Harbour Marina, Hatchet Bay Marina, Harbour Island Marina, Spanish Wells Marine, Spanish Wells Yacht Haven and Valentine's Yacht Club and Inn.

Exuma
Compass Cay Marina, Exuma Docking Service; Farmer's Cay, Highborne Cay, Minns Water Sports and Marine Supplies, Sampson Cay and Staniel Cay.

Grand Bahama
Bell Channel Club and Marina, Harbour Hotel and Marina, Lucayan Marina Village, Marina at Old Bahama Bay, Ocean Reef Yacht Club and Marina, Port Lucaya Marina, Port Lucaya Yacht Club, Running Mon Marina, West End Marina, Xanadu Beach Marina,

Great Guana Cay
Guana Beach Resort and Marina.

Green Turtle Cay
Black Sound Marina, Bluff House Club and Marina, Green Turtle Club and Yacht Club, Other Shore Club and marina.

Long Island
Clarence Town Dock, Flying Fish Marina, Harding's Supplies Center, Stella Maris Marina

Man-O-War-Cay
Man-O-War Marina

New Providence Island
Brown's Boat Basin, Claridge Marina, East Bay Yacht Basin, Lyford Cay Club, Nassau Harbour Club, Nassau Yacht Haven, and Hurricane Hole Marina.

San Salvador
Riding Rock Inn and Marina

Spanish Cay
Spanish Cay Marina.

Treasure Cay
Treasure Cay Beach Hotel and Marina

Walker's Cay
Walker's Cay Hotel Marina

Charter Boat rentals are widely available and include:

Grand Bahama
Grand Bahama Boat Rentals ☎ 373-9153

Ocean Reef Yacht Club ☎ 373-4661

Paradise Watersports ☎ 352-2887

Reef Tours ☎ 373-5880

Viva Cruises ☎ 373-7226

New Providence Island
Barefoot Sailing Cruises ☎ 393-0820

Born Free ☎ 393-4144

Brown's Charters ☎ 324-2061

Chubasco Charters ☎ 322-8148

Coral Reef ☎ 394-4096

Kingfisher ☎ 393-3739

Eleuthera
Charter Cats of the Bahamas ☎ 1-800-446-9441.

GETTING TO THE BAHAMAS

By air

From the US -There are international airports at Nassau on New Providence, and Freeport/Lucaya, Exuma. Abaco, Bimini and San Salvador, with arrivals from most of the major US gateways, including Atlanta, Boston, Chicago, Miami and New York.

American Eagle flies daily from Miami, and with American Airlines offers connections with many US cities. Comair flies from Orlando and Fort Lauderdale daily, with Delta connections to many US cities. Gulf Stream flies daily from Miami and Fort Lauderdale. There are charters from Boston, Newark, Philadelphia/Baltimore, Fort Lauderdale, Chicago Hartford, Cleveland, Cincinnati, Richmond and Raleigh/Durham.

From Canada – Air Canada flies from Montreal and Toronto to Nassau, and a number of charter companies also offer flights from these two cities.

From Europe – British Airways is the only operator flying direct scheduled services from London's Gatwick to Nassau. There are other direct weekly services to Nassau from Frankfurt by Condor and AOM from Paris. Air Europe flies once a week from Italy to Eleuthera and Grand Bahama Island. There are, however, direct scheduled services from most major European airports to Miami with connecting flights for the 35 minute hop across to The Bahamas. There are also convenient connecting flights from New York for trans-Atlantic passengers. It is 2.5 hours flying time from New York, and about 3.5 hours from Toronto.

Both Nassau and Freeport also provide connections for inter-island services operated by Bahamasair, the national carrier. There are more than 50 airports and airstrips throughout the islands of The Bahamas, of which almost half are ports of entry. Pan Am Air Bridge offers an unusual and fascinating seaplane service between Watson Island, close to Miami, and many of the islands of The Bahamas. There are also plenty of light aircraft for charter, and it may even work out cheaper for a party to charter their own small plane than travel by a scheduled flight.

Sea

The Bahamas have long been a major cruise ship destination, and now attract about 1.5 million passengers a year. The islands are visited by all the major cruise lines, and up to seven cruise vessels can be docked in Nassau at any one time, although the facility can handle a maximum of 12 ships. Main cruise lines include Caribbean Line, Carnival, Celebrity, Discovery, Disney, Dolphin, Fantasy, Holland America, Kloster, Norwegian, Premier, Princess, Seascape and Royal Caribbean. There is a high-speed ferry between Miami and Nassau and Miami and Freeport/Lucaya on Grand Bahama, and many ports of entry for yachts.

ARRIVAL, ENTRY REQUIREMENTS AND CUSTOMS

An immigration card has to be filled in and presented on arrival. The form requires you to say where you will be staying on the island, so if you plan to move around, put down the first hotel where you will be staying. The immigration form is in two parts, one of which is stamped and returned to you in your passport. You must retain this until departure when the slip is retrieved as you check in at the airport.

Visitors from the US staying less than 8 months need some form of ID such as a valid passport, or birth certificate that proves citizenship, together with a photo ID, such as driver's licence. Visitors from Canada staying for three weeks or less can also enter by producing valid ID that proves citizenship plus photo ID. All other visitors require a full passport, and some nationals may require a visa, so check in your home country. You must also be in possession of a return air ticket.

If you are on business, a letter confirming this may prove helpful in speeding your way through customs, especially if you are carrying samples.

Having cleared immigration, you will have to go through customs, where you have to make an oral declaration about whether you have goods to declare or not. You may be asked to open your luggage for inspection. If you have expensive cameras, jewelry etc. it is a good idea to travel with a photocopy of the receipt. The duty free allowance entering The Bahamas is 200 cigarettes or 100 cigars (not Cuban) or 1lb of tobacco, two liters (litres) of spirits and reasonable personal effects.

US citizens are allowed to take back up to US$600 worth of duty free goods if out of the country for more than 48 hours. The next US$1,000 is dutiable at 10%, although gifts up to the value of US$50 can be mailed home duty-free. US visitors are also allowed as part of the duty-free allowance, five cartons of cigarettes and one liter (litre) of wine, liqueur or spirits (two liters (litres) if one liter was made in The Bahamas or the Caribbean). US Customs officials are based in The Bahamas and US citizens must clear them before departure.

Canadian citizens are allowed to take back $300 worth of duty free goods if away for a week or more, as well as 200 cigarettes or equivalent, and 40 ounces of alcoholic drinks.

AIRLINES/AIRPORTS

Note: All exchanges are 242 unless stated otherwise

Aerojet	☎ (305) 772-5070
Air Canada	☎ 1-800-776-3000
Air Jamaica	☎ 1-800-523-5585
Air Link	☎ (407) 283-1300
American Airlines/American Eagle	☎ 1-800-433-7300/352-5415

Bahamasair	☎ 1-800-222-4262/357-5771/ 377-5505
British Airways	☎ 1-800-247-9297
Cherokee Air (charters)	☎ 367-2089
Cleare Air (charters)	☎ 377-0341
Congo Air (charters)	☎ 377-5382
Delta/Comair	☎ 352-3070/1-800-221-1212
Dolphin Atlantic (Florida based charters)	☎ 1-800-353-8010
Flamingo Air	☎ 351-4963
Gulfstream Airlines	☎ 377-4314
Island Air Charters (Florida based charters)	☎ 954-359-9942 and 1-800-444-9904
Island Express	☎ (954) 359-0380
Island Ranger Helitours (charters)	☎ 363-1040
Laker Airways	☎ (305) 359-0199/352-3389/ 1-800-422-7466
Major Air	☎ 352-5778
Miami Air Charter	☎ 1-800-333-4698 or (305) 251-9649
Pan Am Air Bridge	☎ 1-800-424-2557 and 377-6449
Paradise Helicopters	☎ 363-4016
Taino Air	☎ 352-8885
Trans Caribbean Air (Florida based charters)	☎ 954-434-5271
Twin Air	☎ 954-359-8266
US Air Express	☎ 1-800-622-1015/949-7488
Walker's International	☎ 1-800-925-5377 or (954) 359-1400

AMERICAN EXPRESS

The American Express office is in Shirley Street, Nassau ☎ 322-2931 or 1-800-528-2121, and 19-20 Regent Centre, Freeport ☎ 352-4444.

BANKS

Banks are open Monday to Thursday from 9.30am to 3pm, and from 9.30am to 5pm on Friday in Nassau, Paradise Island, Cable Beach and Freeport/Lucaya, but hours vary on the Out Islands.
    ATM machines are available on most of the larger islands, airport terminals and casinos.

Out Islands

There are banks in:
Hope Town, Man-O-War Cay, Marsh Harbour, New Plymouth and Treasure Cay. Most are only open Monday to Thursday between

9am and 3pm and on Friday from 9am to 5pm.

San Andros, opens only on Wednesday between 10.30am and 2.30pm.

Alice town North Bimini, open Monday to Friday from 9am to 3pm.

Eleuthera Governor's Harbour. There are two banks that open Monday to Thursday from 9am to 5pm, and on Friday from 9.30am to 5pm.

Rock Sound, open from Monday to Thursday between 9am and 3pm, and on Friday between 9am and 5pm.

BEACHES/SWIMMING

The Bahamas has fabulous beaches, everything you ever dreamed of for a tropical island, miles of sand, a fringe of tall palms for shade, and turquoise calm, clear warm seas. The beaches are clean, litter free and on the Out Islands, usually near-deserted.

Grand Bahama: Barbary, Fortune, Gold Rock, Silver Point, Taino, William's Town and Xanadu.

New Providence: Adelaide Beach, Cable Beach, Cabes Beach, Lighthouse Beach, Love Beach, Orange Hill Beach, Paradise Beach, Saunders Beach and Yamacraw

Out Islands: Almost every beach is idyllic.

BICYCLES

Bikes can be rented at or near most major hotels. Rates start from around $10 a day.

BOOKSTORES

Nassau

Island Book Shop, Bay St.
Lee's Book Centre, Parliament Street.
Nassau Stationers, Rosetta Street.
United Book Shops, Palmdale Shopping Plaza.

Grand Bahama

Bellevue Gifts and Supplies, Queen's Highway, Freeport .
Bahamian Tings, Poplar Crescent, Freeport.

CAMPING

Camping is not allowed.

CAR RENTAL/DRIVING

Cars, jeeps and other 4-wheel drive vehicles can be hired and provide the best way of exploring the island. If you plan to go at

Above & below: Learn to dive and swim with dolphins

Opposite page; Top: Pirates of Nassau Middle: Reef diving, Grand Bahama Below: Munjack Cay, Abaco

Fact File

peak periods, it is best to hire your vehicle in advance through your travel agent. Cars can be hired, however, at airports, hotels or car hire offices on the island. A home driving license, or international driving licence, is valid provided you are not staying for more than three months.

Hire car rates vary enormously but start from around US$40 a day for compact automatics during the summer low season. Winter rates are higher, usually from about US$5-10 a day more. There is quite a wide range of vehicles available and rates depend both on the type of vehicle and the rental company. There are usually quite a lot of incentives, so it pays to shop around.

DRIVE ON THE LEFT and observe the speed limits.

Driving under the influence of alcohol or drugs is against the law, and there are heavy penalties if convicted, especially if it results in an accident.

Avoid clearly marked 'no parking' zones or you might pick up a ticket, but parking generally does not pose a problem.

If you have an accident or breakdown during the day, call your car hire company so make sure you have the telephone number with you. They will usually send out a mechanic or a replacement vehicle. If you are stuck at night make sure the car is off the road, lock the vehicle and call a taxi to take you back to your hotel. Report the problem to the car hire company or the police as soon as possible.

Hire companies include:

Nassau

Avis	☎ 326-6380
Budget	☎ 377-7405
Dollar	☎ 377-7231
Herts	☎ 377-8684

Grand Bahama

Avis	☎ 352-7666
Cartwright's	☎ 351-3002
Courtesy Rental	☎ 352-5212
Dollar	☎ 352-9325/ 5480
Hertz	☎ 353-9277
KSR	☎ 351-5737

Abaco

A & A Cars	☎ 367-2148
H & L Cars	☎ 367-2840
T& B Cars	☎ 367-4007
V & R Cars	☎ 367-2001
Reliable Car Rentals	☎ 367-4234

Andros

Rahmig's Car Rental	☎ 369-1608

Eleuthera

Cash's Taxi and Car Rental	☎ 335-1096
Hilton Johnson Taxi and Car Rental	☎ 335-6241
Neville Major Taxi and Car Rental	☎ 333-2361
Tommy Pinder Taxi and Car Rental	☎ 332-2568
Wilfred Major Taxi and Car Rental	☎ 334-2156
Winsett Cooper Taxi and Car Rental	☎ 332-1592

Exuma

BGS Investments	☎ 336-2122
Exuma Transport	☎ 336-2101

Note: Motor scooters can be hired and the wearing of crash helmets is compulsory. Rates start from about $30 a day but negotiate and you may get a better deal.

CHURCHES

Most people attend church and very many religious denominations are represented with Protestants forming the largest group. Faiths represented include Anglican, Assemblies of Brethren, Assembly of God, Baha'i, Baptist, Christian Science, Church of Christ, Church of God, Church of God of Prophecy, Greek Orthodox, Hebrew, Islam, Jehovah's Witness, Lutheran, Mennonite, Methodist, Mormon, Pentecostal, Presbyterian, Roman Catholic, Salvation Army and Seventh Day Adventist.

For further information about times of services ring:

Grand Bahama

Anglican	☎ 352-5402
Baptist	☎ 352-9224
Methodist	☎ 373-5752
Presbyterian	☎ 373-2568
Roman Catholic	☎ 273-3300
Salvation Army	☎ 352-4863

New Providence Island

Anglican	☎ 322-4186/ 8220
Baptist	☎ 325-3556
Methodist	☎ 325-2552/ 393-2936
Presbyterian	☎ 393-2534
Roman Catholic	☎ 323-3802
Salvation Army	☎ 393-2340.

CLOTHING

Casual and comfortable are the keywords but you can generally be as smart or as cool as you like. A number of restaurants and clubs have dress codes, and if you plan to visit these, you should pack accordingly. Beachwear is fine for the beach and pool areas, but cover up a little for the street. Informal is the order of the day and night, and this is not the place for suits and ties or evening gowns, unless you really like dressing up for dinner or are staying at a very smart hotel. During the day, light cotton, casual clothes are ideal for exploring in. During the evening, a light jumper or wrap may sometimes be needed. It is fun to change for dinner, but for men this normally means smart slacks or trousers, and for women a summer dress or similar. There are establishments, however, where sports coats or jackets are not out of place and some smarter restaurants prefer them in the evening while women can be as elegant as they wish.

If you plan to explore on foot, stout footwear and a good water-proof jacket are essential. Also, wear sunglasses and a hat to protect you from the sun during the hottest part of the day, and you will need sandals on the beach, as the sand can get too hot to walk in bare feet.

CURRENCY

The official currency on the island is the Bahamian dollar (B$) that is pegged to and keeps the same value as the US dollar. US dollars are accepted everywhere on the islands, and change can be given

in either or both currencies. Of interest are the Bahamian $3 and Quincentennial $1 notes and the square 15c coin. Other notes come in 50c, $1, $5, $10, $20, $50 and $100 values.

The banks offer a fixed rate of exchange which is usually better than that offered by hotels. Traveler's checks (travellers cheques), preferably in US dollars, are also accepted in hotels and large stores, and all major credit cards can be used in hotels, dive and watersports businesses, many stores and restaurants. It is best to spend all your Bahamian dollars while on the islands because you will not get such a favorable rate if you exchange them back home.

Note: Always have a few small denomination notes for tips.

DEPARTURE TAX

There is a B$15 departure tax for all visitors over the age of six (BB$18 from Freeport).

DRUGS

There are strict laws prohibiting the possession and use of drugs, including marijuana. Heavy fines and prison await those who ignore the law.

ELECTRICITY

The usual electricity supply is 120 volts, 60 cycles AC that is suitable for US appliances. Adaptors are necessary for European appliances without dual voltages.

EMBASSIES

Canada – Nassau   ☎ 393-2123
UK – Nassau   ☎ 325-7471
US – Nassau   ☎ 322-1181

EMERGENCY TELEPHONE NUMBERS

For Police, Fire and Ambulance dial 919
    Also Nassau ☎ 322-4444, Grand Bahama ☎ 352-8352
    or Ambulance – Grand Bahama ☎ 352-2689, New Providence Island ☎ 322-2221
    Bahamas Air Sea Rescue (BASRA) ☎ 322-3877 New Providence and ☎ 352-6222 on Grand Bahama.

ESSENTIAL THINGS TO PACK

Sun block, cream, sunglasses, sun hat, camera (and lots of film), insect repellant, binoculars (if interested in birding and wildlife) and a small flashlight in case of power failures.

FACILITIES FOR DISABLED PERSONS

Many of the watersports and dive operations will accommodate disabled visitors. There are some facilities for the disabled at most of the larger resorts.

FESTIVALS/PUBLIC HOLIDAYS *

January

New Year's Day * and Junkanoo Parades
New Year's Day Cruising Regattas, Exuma
Bahamas International Windsurfing Regatta

February

Annual Farmer's Cay Festival, Exuma
Archives Annual Exhibition, Nassau
Ash Wednesday (date varies)
Heart Ball, Nassau
Nassau Cup Yacht Race

March/April

Good Friday *(date varies)
Easter Monday *(date varies)
Annual George Town Cruising Regatta
Annual Family Island Regatta, George Town
Annual Red Cross Fair, Government House Grounds

May

Annual Green Turtle Club Fishing Tournament, Green Turtle Cay
Annual Long Island Regatta and visiting yachts parade

June

Labor Day – First Friday *
Whit Monday (seven weeks after Easter) *
Eleuthera Pineapple Festival

July

Bahama Cup (sailing)
Abaco Regatta
Annual Staniel Cay Bonefish Tournament
10 July Independence Day, part of a week of festivities *

August

Emancipation Day First Monday *

October

12 October Discovery Day *
Annual McLean's Town Conch Cracking Contest
North Eleuthera Regatta

Fact File

November

Remembrance Day

December

Sun International Bahamas Open (tennis)
Annual New Plymouth Historical Cultural Weekend
Annual Beaux Arts Masked Ball
Junior Junkanoo Parade
25th Christmas Day *
26th Boxing Day * and Junkanoo Parade
New Year's Eve

GALLERIES

Grand Bahama

Bahama Art
Sun Coral Plaza
☎ 373-6870

Bahamian Tings
Poplar Crescent
☎ 352-9550

Flovin Gallery and Craft
International Bazaar
☎ 352-7564

Freeport Art Centre
Queens Highway
☎ 351-4603

New Providence Island

**Andrew Aitken
Frame Art Gallery**
Madeira Street
☎ 328-7065

Balmain Antiques
Bay Street
☎ 323-7421

Caripelago
Bay Street
☎ 326-3568

**Central Bank of
Bahamas Art Gallery**
Market Street
☎ 322-2193

Chan Pratt's Art Gallery
Bonney Way
☎ 364-4047

Charlotte's gallery
Charlotte Street
☎ 322-6310

**European Art Museum
and Gallery**
East Bay Street
☎ 393-4711

Kennedy Gallery
Parliament Street
☎ 325-7662

Kye Shon Gallery
Frederick Street
☎ 322-5007

Lyford Cay Gallery
Lyford Cay
☎ 362-4034

Marlborough Antiques
Marlborough Street
☎ 328-0502

Nassau Art Gallery
East Bay Shopping Centre
☎ 393-1482

Nassau Glass Company
Mackey Street
☎ 393-8165

Paradise Tees
Hurricane Hole Plaza
☎ 363-2609

The Plait Lady
Bay Street and Victoria Avenue
☎ 356-5584

GAMBLING

There are four casinos:
Crystal Palace Resort and Casino, Cable Beach
Lucayan Beach Resort and Casino, Lucaya
Atlantis Resort and Casino, Paradise Island
Princess Casino in Freeport.

Guests must be over 18 to gamble. Casinos are usually open during the day for gaming and some are open 24 hours for the slot machines. The casinos also hold sessions to teach the rudiments of the various games of chance.

HEALTH

There are no serious health problems although visitors should take precautions against the sun, which can ruin your holiday. Immunization is not required unless coming from an infected area. All hotels have doctors either resident or on call, and standards of health care are high.

The main hospitals in Nassau are:
Princess Margaret Hospital, Shirley Street, ☎ 322-2861
Doctor's Hospital, Shirley Street, ☎ 322-8411.

There are clinics throughout the island and a number of pharmacies.

Grand Bahama

The main health care facility is the Rand Memorial Hospital, East Atlantic Drive, ☎ 352-6735. Other facilities include two Lucayan Medical Centres, ☎ 352-7288, and Sunrise Medical Centre, ☎ 373-3333.

There are medical services available on the following Out Islands:

Abaco
Abaco Clinic
☎ 367-4240

Cooper's Town Clinic
☎ 365-0019

Government Clinic
☎ 367-2510

Great Abaco Clinic
☎ 367-2320

Hope Town Clinic
☎ 366-0108

Moore Island Clinic
☎ 366-6105

Sandy Point Clinic
☎ 366-4010

Treasure Cay
☎ 365-8288

Andros
Central Andros Clinic
☎ 368-2038

Fresh Creek Clinic
☎ 368-2038

Kemp's Bay Clinic
☎ 369-1849

Nicholl's Town Clinic
☎ 329-2055

Mangrove Cay Clinic
☎ 309-0089

Mastic Point Clinic
☎ 329-3055.

Bimini

Clinic ☎ 347-3210

Cat Island

Arthur' Town, Old Bight, Smith Bay (no telephones)

Eleuthera

Harbour Island Medical Clinic
☎ 333-2225

Governor's Harbour
☎ 332-2774

Rock Sound Medical Clinic
☎ 334-2226

Exuma

Black Point Clinic
☎ 355-3007

Farmer's Cay Clinic
☎ 355-4015

George Town Clinic
☎ 336-2088

Island Clinic
☎ 356-2022

Steventon Clinic
☎ 358-0053

Inagua

Great Inagua Clinic

San Salvador

The Clinic

Tanning safely

The sun is very strong but sea breezes often disguise just how hot it is. If you are not used to the sun, take it carefully for the first two or three days, use a good sunscreen with a factor of 15 or higher, and do not sunbathe during the hottest parts of the day. Wear sunglasses and a sun hat. Sunglasses will protect you against the glare, especially strong on the beach, and sun hats will protect your head.

If you spend a lot of time swimming or scuba diving, take extra care, as you will burn even more quickly because of the combination of salt water and sun. Calamine lotion and preparations containing aloe are both useful in combating sunburn.

Irritating insects

Mosquitoes are not usually a problem on or near the beaches because of onshore winds, but they may well bite you as you enjoy an open-air evening meal. Use a good insect repellant, particularly if you are planning trips inland. Lemon grass can sometimes be found growing naturally, and a handful of this in your room is also a useful mosquito deterrent.

Sand flies can be a problem on the beach. Despite their tiny size they can give you a nasty bite. And, ants exist, so make sure you check the ground carefully before sitting down otherwise you might get bitten, and the bites can itch for days.

Note: Drinking water from the tap is generally safe although it is advisable to check with your hotel reception in case of any local problems. Bottled mineral and distilled water is widely available.

Fact File

HURRICANES

Hurricane season is between June and November with August, September and early October the most likely months for tropical storms, although thankfully, most of these pass safely well north of the islands. Weather stations track all tropical storms and give considerable warning of likely landfall.

LANGUAGE

The official language is English, although with a lilting accent. French is spoken by Haitian immigrants who also have their own Creole dialect.

LOST PROPERTY

Report lost property as soon as possible to your hotel or the nearest police station.

MEDIA

The *Nassau Guardian*, founded in 1844, is the daily morning paper, and the *Tribune* is the daily evening. On Grand Bahama, there is the *Freeport News* and *Grand Bahama News*. Most major US and foreign papers and magazines are widely available on the main islands.

NIGHTLIFE

The Bahamas offer a great choice of entertainment from great dining to live theatre and comedy clubs, and karaoke bars to cabaret. Many of the larger hotels and resorts offer live entertainment, and there are bars, dancing and discos. And, for something really exciting, experience a night dive.

PERSONAL INSURANCE AND MEDICAL COVER

Make sure you have adequate personal insurance and medical cover. If you need to call out a doctor or have medical treatment, you will probably have to pay for it at the time, so keep all receipts so that you can reclaim on your insurance.

Fact File

PHARMACIES

There are a number of pharmacies in both Nassau and Freeport/ Lucaya, and many can be found in the shopping arcades of the larger hotels.

PHOTOGRAPHY

The intensity of the sun can play havoc with your films, especially if photographing near water or white sand. Compensate for the brightness otherwise your photographs will come out over exposed and washed out. The heat can actually damage film so store reels in a box or bag in the hotel fridge if there is one. Also remember to protect your camera if on the beach, as a single grain of sand is all it takes to jam your camera.

It is very easy to get 'click happy', but be tactful and polite when taking photographs. Many islanders are shy or simply fed up with being photographed. You will have to decide whether the picture is worth it, but if a person declines to have their photograph taken, do not ignore this. The islanders are a warm and very hospitable race and if you stop and spend some time finding out what they are doing, they will usually then allow you to take a photograph.

POLICE

Police Headquarters in Nassau is in East Hill Street ☎ 322-4444, and in the International Building, West Mall Drive, Freeport ☎ 352-8352.

PORTS

The main ports are Prince George Dock, Nassau ☎ 326-7354, and Freeport Harbour ☎ 352-9651/9163.

POST OFFICE

In Nassau and Freeport, the post offices are open from Monday to Friday between 8.30am and 5.30pm, and in Nassau only, to 12.30pm on Saturday. Post Offices on the Out Islands are often open only a few days of the week, but hotels and many shops sell stamps.

The General Post Office in Nassau is in East Hill Street ☎ 322-3344, and in Freeport in Explorers Way ☎ 352-8044.

PUBLIC TOILETS

There are not many public toilets on the island, but bars, restaurants and hotels have private facilities that can usually be used if you ask politely.

RESTAURANTS

There is a remarkably large choice when it comes to eating out on the island. There are the inevitable fast food burger, pizza and fried chicken outlets, beach cafés offering excellent value for money, and elegant dining rooms, as well as restaurants offering a wide range of ethnic cuisines, from Caribbean cooking to Chinese. Most accept credit cards and during peak times of the year, reservations are recommended. If you come across a restaurant not listed in the guide, or have comments about any of those that are, I would very much like to hear from you.

Some restaurants are closed on Saturday for lunch and all day Sunday, but hotel restaurants are open daily and welcome outside guests. The restaurants listed in the itineraries are classified by price – $ inexpensive, $$ moderate, $$$ expensive.

SECURITY

The Bahamas have little serious crime but it makes sense like anywhere else, not to walk around wearing expensive items or flashing large sums of money. Secure your valuables, as you should anywhere, and do not leave items unattended on the beach or in an unlocked car.

Don't carry around your passport, travelers checks (travellers cheques) or all your money. Keep them secure in your room or in a hotel safety deposit box. It is also a good idea to have photocopies of the information page of your passport, your air ticket and holiday insurance policy. All will help greatly if the originals are lost.

The islanders are genuinely warm and friendly and very laid back, so there is little hard sell and they will go to great lengths to make your visit memorable.

SERVICE CHARGES AND TAXES

There is a Government tax of 4% and a 4% hotel tax on accommodation bills, and some add an extra 2% as an 'energy' tax, as well as automatically adding up to 5% for staff tips.

A 10-15% service charge may also be added to restaurant bills. Menus and tariffs sometimes include these charges so check to make sure they have not been added again. In shops, the price on the label is what you pay.

SHELLS

Shells are washed up on to the beaches of the Bahamas but they should be left for others to enjoy.

SHOPPING

Shops are usually open from Monday to Saturday between 9am

Fact File

and 5pm, although some close one afternoon during the week while the larger shopping malls are open until 8pm.

The Bahamas offer excellent shopping from top name designer clothes, to fine china and crystal, perfumes and jewels, especially that made from black coral. The best shopping is in Nassau, Cable Beach, Paradise Island and Freeport/Lucaya, although there are boutiques and gift shops in all resorts.

Best buys include: duty free goods, local arts and crafts, clothing, island music tapes.

SIGHTSEEING/TOURS

Sightseeing and island tours by land or sea can be organized through hotels, tour representatives or one of the many specialist tour companies on the islands. Only Ministry of Tourism licensed guides are allowed into historical sites.

These include:

Nassau

Aarow Travel and Tours
☎ 393-1981

Cable Beach Travel
☎ 327-2049

Fiesta Travel
☎ 325-8434

First Class Travel
☎ 322-7127

Five Star Travel
☎ 356-6140

Island Sun Tours
☎ 325-695

Island Vacations
☎ 356-1111

Miracle Tours
☎ 326-0283

Mundy Tours
☎ 393-6900

New Providence Travel
☎ 328-2868

Paradise Travel
☎ 325-0810

Park Place Travel and Tours
☎ 356-5063

Premier Travel
☎ 328-0264

Stuart's Tour and Travel
Service, ☎ 325-7122

Superior Travel
☎ 327-7212

Tropical Travel Tours
☎ 322-4091

United Travel
☎ 394-8747

V&B Travel Tours
☎ 356-6170

World Executive Travel
☎ 325-0810

Grand Bahama

Bahama Dreams
☎ 351-7099

Bain's Travel
☎ 352-3861

Best Island Tours
☎ 351-4409

Deep Star Submarine
☎ 373-8940

Island Fun and Sun
☎ 351-4000

East End Adventures
☎ 373-6662

Kayak Nature Tours
☎ 373-2485

Executive Tours
☎ 373-7863

Reef Tours
☎ 373-5880

Forbes Charter Services
☎ 352-9311

Sun World Travel and Tours
☎ 352-3717

TELEPHONES

There are good international telephone, fax and cable services on all the main islands provided by The Bahamas Telecommunications Service (Batelco), although radio communication is used on some of the smallest Out Islands and calls may take a little longer to get through. For the operator dial 0, for directory assistance dial 916. Remember that direct dialing from your hotel room may still incur a hefty surcharge, and it is usually much cheaper to ring from a Batelco office.

The international code for The Bahamas is 242. From the US, dial 1-242 and the seven-digit island number.

From the UK and Europe, dial 001-242 and the seven-digit island number. From the Bahamas to ring the US, dial 1 + area code + seven digit local number. AT&T's USA DIRECT calling service is available. To connect the AT&T operator on The Bahamas, dial 1-800-872-2881.

To ring the UK, dial 011-44-area code and then the local number.

TIME

The Bahamas operate under Eastern Standard Time (EST) that is five hours behind GMT from October to when the clocks go forward in March. Eastern Daylight Time operates between March and when the clocks go back in October.

TIPPING

Tips are generally added to restaurant bills but check in case it is not. It is customary to tip bellhops in hotels, taxi drivers, guides and other people providing a service. Tip taxi drivers around 10-15% and bell hops $1-2 for each piece of luggage.

TOURIST OFFICES

There are tourist information centers in:

Grand Bahama

Freeport International Airport
☎ 352-2052

International Bazaar
☎ 352-6909

Port Lucaya
☎ 373-8988

New Providence Island

Two at the International Airport, open daily from 8.30am to 11pm, and at Rawson Square and Market Plaza, both open daily from 8.30am to 5pm.

Overseas, there are Bahamas Tourist Offices in:

USA

150 East 52 Street, 28th floor, New York NY 10022.
☎ 212-758-2777

3450 Wilshire Boulevard, Suite 208, Los Angeles, CA 90010, ☎ 213-385-0033

19495 Biscayne Boulevard, Suite 809, Aventura Fl 33180,
☎ 305-932-0051

8600 W. Bryn Mawr Avenue, Suite 820, Chicago, Il 60631,
☎ 312-693-1114

Bahama Out Islands Promotion Board

1100 Lee Wagener Boulevard, Suite 206, Fort Lauderdale, Fl 33315, ☎ 305-359-8099.

2050 Stemmons Freeway, Suite 116, Dallas, Texas 75258-1408 ☎ 214-742-1886

Canada

121 Bloor Street East, Suite 1101, Toronto ON M4W 3M5,
☎ 416-968-2999

UK

3 The Billings, Walnut Tree Close, Guildford, Surrey GU1 4UL. ☎ 01483-448900

France

60 rue Saint Lazare, 75009 Paris ☎ 45-26-6262

Germany

Leipziger Strasse 67d, 60487 Frankfurt/Main-70
☎ 49-69-970-8340

Italy

Via Cusani 7, 20121 Milan
☎ 7202-3003/2526

WEDDINGS

The Bahamas are increasingly becoming a popular destination for honeymoon couples, and other couples get carried away by the romance of the islands and decide to marry while on vacation. It is believed the first foreigners to choose The Bahamas for their wedding were a Japanese couple who were married in 1985 in the historic Christ Church Cathedral. If you decide to marry, you can enjoy a traditional church ceremony, or make your vows on the beach, on a luxury yacht or in a flower-bedecked gazebo by a sparkling hotel pool.

Getting married involves some very simple steps. These include:

Both parties must be in the Commonwealth of The Bahamas at the time of application.

The couple must have resided in The Bahamas not less than 15 days prior to the date of application, although the Register General has certain discretion in this, and a letter accompanying the application would normally get a waiver provided both parties have resided in The Bahamas for three days.

If either party has been divorced, a final decree or certified copy must be produced.

A license application fee of B$40 must be paid.

Blood tests are not required, and couples wishing to marry on one of the Out Islands should apply to the Office of the Administrator on the island where they wish to be wed, although marriage licenses are issued at the office of the Register General, Rodney Bain Building, Parliament and Shirley Streets, Nassau, which is open from Monday to Friday between 9.30am and 4.30pm. The Register General, PO Box H-5553, Nassau, Bahamas, ☎ 322-5553.

There are Administrators on the following Out Islands: Abaco, Andros, Berry Islands, Bimini, Cat Island, Crooked Island, Eleuthera, Exuma, Harbour Island, Long Island, Inagua, Mayaguana, San Salvador and Rum Cay.

Many hotels on Grand Bahama and New Providence Island offer special wedding and honeymoon packages and have experts available to help you with all the planning. Or, you may contact the Ministry of Tourism in Nassau ☎ 302-2034 or the Grand Bahama Island Tourism Board ☎ 352-8044/5, where a wedding coordinator will assist you in arranging the perfect wedding. This is a complimentary service.

Out Island hotels offering honeymoon packages include:

Abaco

Abaco Inn

Bluff House Club and Marina

Green Turtle Yacht Club, Guana Beach Resort and Marina

Hope Town Harbour Lodge

Inn at Spanish Cay, Pelican Beach Villas

Sea Spray Resort and Villas

Walker's Cay Hotel and Marina.

Andros

Emerald Palms By The Sea

Bimini

Bimini Big Game Fishing Club and Hotel

Cat Island

Fernandez Bay Village

Eleuthera

Cotton Bay Club, Cove Eleuthera

Exuma

Coconut Cove

Club Peace and Plenty

Peace and Plenty Beach Inn

Harbour Island

Coral Sands Hotel

Romora Bay Club

Long Island

Stella Maris Resort Club

LANDMARK
VISITORS GUIDES

US & British Virgin Islands

US & British VI*
ISBN: 1 901522 03 2
256pp,
UK £11.95 US $15.95

Antigua & Barbuda

Antigua & Barbuda*
ISBN: 1 901522 02 4
96pp,
UK £5.95 US $12.95

Bermuda

Bermuda*
ISBN: 1 901522 07 5
160pp,
UK £7.95 US $12.95

Barbados

Barbados*
ISBN: 1 901522 32 6
144pp,
UK £6.95 US $12.95

St Lucia

St Lucia*
ISBN: 1 901522 82 2
144pp,
UK £6.95 US $13.95

Pack 2 months into 2 weeks with your Landmark Visitors Guides

Jamaica

Jamaica*
ISBN: 1 901522 31 8
144pp
UK £6.95 US $12.95

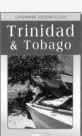

Trinidad & Tobago

Trinidad & Tobago*
ISBN: 1 901522 05 9
160pp,
UK £7.95 US $12.95

Florida: Gulf Coast

Florida: Gulf Coast*
ISBN: 1 901522 01 6
160pp
UK £7.95 US $12.95

Florida: The Keys

Florida: The Keys*
ISBN: 1 901522 21 0
160pp,
UK £7.95 US $12.95

Orlando & Central Florida

Orlando*
ISBN: 1 901522 22 9
256pp,
UK £9.95 US $15.95

Dominican Republic

Dominican Republic*
ISBN: 1 901522 08 3
160pp,
UK £7.95 US $12.95

Gran Canaria

Gran Canaria*
ISBN: 1 901522 19 9
160pp
UK £7.95 US $12.95

Northern Cyprus

North Cyprus
ISBN: 1 901522 51 2
192pp
UK £8.95

Madeira

Madeira
ISBN: 1 901522 42 3
192pp,
UK £8.95

To order send a cheque (check)/Visa/MasterCard/Switch details to: Landmark Publishing,
Ashbourne Hall, Cokayne Ave, Ashbourne, Derbyshire DE6 IEJ England
Tel: 01335 347349 Fax: 01335 347303
e-mail: landmark@clara.net web site: www.landmarkpublishing.co.uk

* In USA order from **Hunter Publishing**
130 Campus Drive, Edison NJ 08818, Tel (732) 225 1900 or (800) 255 0343
Fax: (732) 417 0482 web site: www.hunterpublishing.com

Provence*
ISBN: 1 901522 45 8
240pp,
UK £10.95 US $17.95

Côte d'Azur*
ISBN: 1 901522 29 6
144pp,
UK £6.95 US $13.95

Dordogne
ISBN: 1 901522 67 9
176pp,
UK £9.95

Vendée
ISBN: 1 901522 76 X
160pp,
UK £7.95

Languedoc
ISBN: 1 901522 79 2
144pp,
UK £6.95

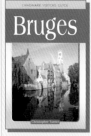

Bruges*
ISBN: 1 901522 66 0
96pp,
UK £5.95 US $10.95

Ticino
ISBN: 1 901522 74 1
192pp
UK £8.95

Italian Lakes*
ISBN: 1 901522 75 X
240pp,
UK £10.95 US $15.95

Riga*
ISBN: 1 901522 59 8
160pp,
UK £7.95

Cracow*
ISBN: 1 901522 54 7
160pp,
UK £7.95

Iceland*
ISBN: 1 901522 68 7
192pp,
UK £12.95 US $17.95

New Zealand*
ISBN: 1 901522 36 9
320pp
UK £12.95 US $18.95

Sri Lanka
ISBN: 1 901522 37 7
192pp,
UK £9.95

India: Kerala
ISBN: 1 901522 16 4
256pp,
UK £10.99

India: Goa
ISBN: 1 901522 23 7
160pp,
UK £7.95

Prices subject to alteration from time to time

INDEX

LANDMARK
VISITORS GUIDES

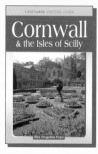

Cornwall
ISBN: 1 901522 09 1
256pp, Full colour
£9.95

Devon
ISBN: 1 901522 42 3
224pp, Full colour
£9.95

Dorset
ISBN: 1 901522 46 6
240pp, Full colour
£9.95

Somerset
ISBN: 1 901522 40 7
224pp, Full colour
£10.95

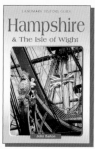
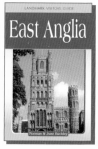

Cotswolds
ISBN: 1 901522 12 1
224pp, Full colour
£9.99

Hampshire
ISBN: 1 901522 14 8
224pp, Full colour
£9.95

East Anglia
ISBN: 1 901522 58 X
224pp, Full colour
£9.95

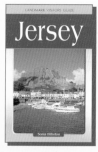
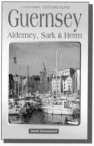
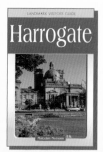

Scotland
ISBN: 1 901522 18 0
288pp, Full colour
£11.95

Jersey
ISBN: 1 901522 47 4
224pp, Full colour
£9.99

Guernsey
ISBN: 1 901522 48 2
224pp, Full colour
£9.95

Harrogate
ISBN: 1 901522 55 5
96pp, Full colour
£4.95